Skinny-dipping in Firesteel Creek and the Jim River was a youthful pleasure for earlier Davison County generations before agricultural runoff and diminished flows of artesian wells and springs changed the character of the streams. Edna Weller collection.

In Participation with Pride

For more than nine decades Commercial Bank has been intimately involved in the affairs of Mitchell and Davison County.

Our founders—Howard R. Kibbee, Sr., George H. Rew, J. T. Morrow and Samuel Webber—established the Commercial Savings Bank of Mitchell on January 6, 1897, with a capital investment of $10,000. Since then our name has been simplified, and in 1993 our assets had increased to more than $153 million.

Having grown with the community we serve, we are proud to join with the Mitchell Area Historical Society as sponsors of this historical trip down Davison County's memory lane.

It is our hope that the book will bring back memories and become a treasured addition to your library.

James D. Hopkins
President

John Philip Sousa and his famous band made their second appearance at the Corn Palace in 1907. In 1904 he was reticent to appear, fearing he might not be paid. Not only did he get his money, but he was delighted with the reception he received. Mitchell Area Historical Society.

An Historic Sampler of

DAVISON COUNTY

by Bob Karolevitz

THE DONNING COMPANY PUBLISHERS

In 1926 Davison County was served by two graveled highways: the east-west U.S. 16 and the north-south State 37. The latter then ran through the town of Ethan. Eventually it was relocated a mile to the west. Vern and Tracy Wittstruck collection.

The Donning Company/Publishers
184 Business Park Drive, Suite 106
Virginia Beach, VA 23462

Steve Mull, General Manager
Bob Johnson, Project Director
Paula M. Foster, Project Research Coordinator
Elizabeth B. Bobbitt, Production Editor
Mary Eliza Midgett, Designer

Library of Congress Cataloging in Publication Data:
Karolevitz, Robert F.
Davison County : an historic sampler / by Bob Karolevitz
p. cm.
Includes bibliographical references and index.
ISBN 0-89865-884-5 (acid-free paper : hardcover)
1. Davison County (S. D.)—History—Pictorial works 2. Davison County (S. D.)—History. I. Title.
F657.D25K37 1993 93-23708
978.3'374—dc20 CIP
Printed in the United States of America

TABLE OF CONTENTS

An Introductory Word 7
Acknowledgments 13
Chapter 1 17
It All Began at Firesteel
Chapter 2 25
Mitchell: A Prairie Boom Town
Chapter 3 35
Land as Rich as the Valley of the Nile
Chapter 4 43
The Refinements of Churches, Schools, and Library Books
Chapter 5 57
A Palace of Corn and a Capital Fight
Chapter 6 79
A Bit of Scandal—and a New Century
Chapter 7 105
The War to End All Wars—and the Tinsel Twenties
Chapter 8 131
Drouth, Debt and Destruction
Chapter 9 149
The Aftermath of War: A New Era
Chapter 10 157
People, Politics and Potpourri
Epilogue 179
Bibliography 184
Index 184
About the Author 192

The dam at White's Mill on the Jim River offered a productive fishing hole for succeeding generations. The mill was built in 1880 and later fell into disrepair. Robert F. McMahon collection.

The Famous
Drum Major
of the
"Kilties".
Mitchell Corn Palace
Sept. 24-29, 1906
RODERICK BAIN MACKENZIE
The Drum Major of the "KILTIES," is celebrated throughout Canada. He is one of the finest specimens of manhood in all Canada, and it is doubtful if a more striking soldier lives. He is seven feet one and a half inches tall.

AN INTRODUCTORY WORD

What you are about to read and to view is not a detailed dates-and-names history of Davison County. Instead, it is what candy-makers used to call a sampler—a flavored taste in words and pictures of a geographic bonbon situated in the heartland of South Dakota. The purpose of this book is not to document first doctor, first teacher, first automobile or other first-on-the scene individuals, institutions or events, but to provide a broad brush, camera's-eye view of the 432-square-mile rectangle of prairie real estate named for a man who has literally disappeared into the cobwebs of the past.

It is, in essence, a pictographic story of pioneer challenges, of successes and failures, of good times and bad as homesteaders broke virgin sod, fortune-seeking entrepreneurs established their various businesses in clapboard shacks until they could build better, and new families on the scene generated an urgent need for churches, schools and other refinements. Genealogical researchers generally will have to look elsewhere for explicit factual data about their Davison County forebears. The book likewise contains no bare lists of teachers, preachers, police chiefs, mayors or other office holders. However, it does depict the ever-changing stage on which succeeding generations pursued their work, their recreation, their cultural diversion and their dreams.

Two key factors—the Homestead Act of 1862 and railroad expansion—played major roles in the settlement of the region and the founding of the currently surviving towns of Mitchell, Ethan and Mount Vernon. Loomis never achieved the expectations of its promoters; Betts lived and died with the railroad; and hopeful postoffices at Rome, Badger, Blendon, Chanka, Emsley, Goshen, Morriston, Stover and Victor came and went, leaving little evidence of their earlier existence.

The principal arteries of transportation—first the railroads and later Interstate 90—have supplied the life blood of the county. They made possible the development of an agricultural economy, eventually supplemented by tourism, educational facilities and manufacturing enterprises. As a result of its location, Mitchell grew into a thriving hub city for a multi-county region; and its unique Corn Palace—widely promoted as the "world's only"—became the area's centerpiece for entertainment, a magnet for camera-clicking visitors and, without question, one of the state's most recognized symbols, second only to the Shrine of Democracy at Mount Rushmore.

1893 Corn Belt Exposition silk badge. Jean Geyerman collection.

Because of its size and its role as the county seat, Mitchell obviously gets the lion's share of attention in this book. However, that doesn't mean that the rest of the county is any less important to this story—or that the author holds a prejudice against the smaller towns or the rural areas. It's mostly just a case of going where the action is.

As with most local histories, many of the "facts" which have been passed down through the years include contradictory details and sometimes obvious errors. These can be attributed generally to faulty memories and occasionally embellishments of pioneers writing or dictating memoirs at a later time. Names of early-day homesteaders and town residents were often spelled in as many as three different ways in the newspapers and on official documents, making it difficult to ascertain the correct one. However, every effort has been made to set the record straight, but with the lack of documentary evidence, it was not always possible to verify reminiscences or to separate reality from legend.

One last note: Because photographs were not always available to match the chronological story, some will appear in this book seemingly out of context. This was a design necessity, and hopefully will not affect the overall acceptance and appreciation of this "sampler."

So, with the limitations mentioned, what follows is a kaleidoscopic view of the second smallest of South Dakota's 66 counties by

Julius L. Corker's candy store and soda fountain in the Crow Building offered Mitchellites everything from gum drops to Green River pop, but very little in customer comfort. Corker is also remembered for his restaurant and popcorn stand. Mitchell Area Historical Society.

size (in a virtual tie with its neighboring twin, Hanson)—but largest by far in the hearts of those who call it home.

Before the horseless carriage took over, bicycles offered a popular means of transportation for Davison County men and women. The high-wheelers were 19th century models. J. Leonard Jennewein photo collection with the N. J. Dunham manuscript, Layne Library, Dakota Wesleyan University.

In the Valley of the Jim

They're a-harvestin' the wheatfields in the Valley of the Jim; I can hear the reapers clatter, soundin' kinda low an' dim. See the yellow fields a-wavin' an' the shocks in crooked rows; An' house, an' barn, an' mother out a-hanging' up the clo'es.See the cattle in the pasture, an' the ole gray limpin' mule, An' the yellow heifer standin' in the water keepin' cool. O, I try to fight agin it as a sort of willy whim— But I wisht 'at I was back there in the Valley of the Jim.

—Will Dillman

Murals in the entryway of the Davison County courthouse were painted by artist Bill Lackey. One depicted early settlers in old Firesteel, the other picnickers and fishermen at White's Mill on the Jim River. Both the courthouse and the art commission were financed by the Works Progress Administration. Clyde Goin photos.

The Friends of the Middle Border Museum received a valuable gift from the renowned artist-illustrator Harvey Dunn in 1944. His "Dakota Woman" was one of a series of nostalgic prairie paintings he produced to depict memories of his youth. Clyde Goin photo.

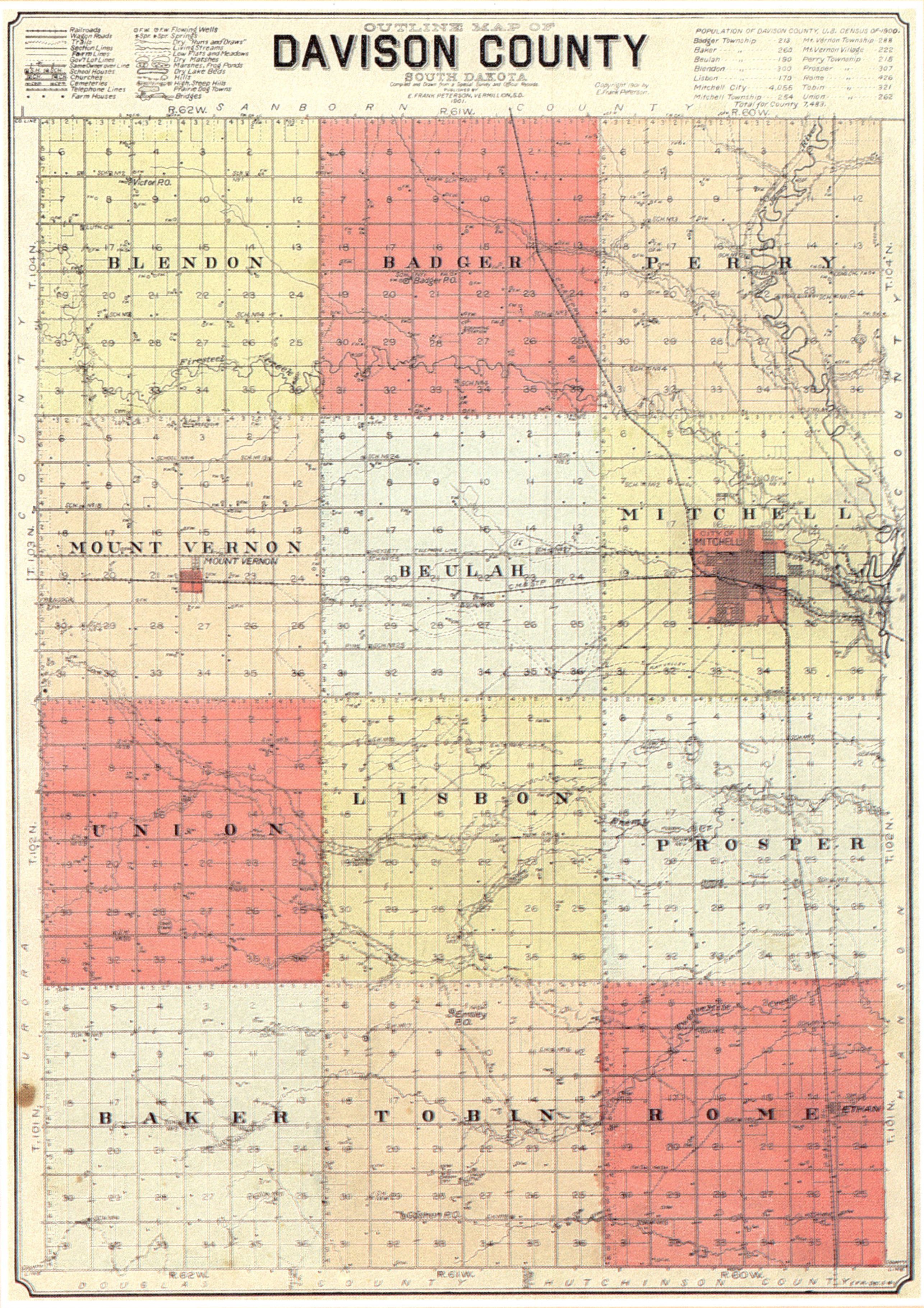

OUTLINE MAP OF
DAVISON COUNTY
SOUTH DAKOTA
Compiled and Drawn from a Special Survey and Official Records
PUBLISHED BY
E. FRANK PETERSON, VERMILLION, S.D.
1901.
Copyright 1901 by E. Frank Peterson.
Railroads
Wagon Roads
Trails
Section Lines
Farm Lines
Gov't Lot Lines
Same Owner over Line
School Houses
Churches
Cemeteries
Telephone Lines
Farm Houses
Flowing Wells
Springs
Dry "Runs and Draws"
Living Streams
Low Flats and Meadows
Dry Marshes
Marshes, Frog Ponds
Dry Lake Beds
Hills
High, Steep Hills
Prairie Dog Towns
Bridges
POPULATION OF DAVISON COUNTY, U.S. CENSUS OF 1900.
Badger Township 213
Baker " 260
Beulah " 190
Blendon " 300
Lisbon " 170
Mitchell City 4,055
Mitchell Township 254
Mt. Vernon Township 288
Mt. Vernon Village 222
Perry Township 215
Prosper " 307
Rome " 426
Tobin " 321
Union " 262
Total for County 7,483.
R.62W. SANBORN R.61W. COUNTY R.60W.
BLENDON
BADGER
PERRY
MOUNT VERNON
BEULAH
MITCHELL
CITY OF MITCHELL
UNION
LISBON
PROSPER
BAKER
TOBIN
ROME
T.104N.
T.103N.
T.102N.
T.101N.
Victor P.O.
Badger P.O.
Firesteel Creek
Ethan
Mount Vernon
R.62W. DOUGLAS R.61W. COUNTY HUTCHINSON R.60W. COUNTY

Photo.

ACKNOWLEDGMENTS

Two organizations deserve credit for the publication of this book: the Commercial Bank of Mitchell and the Mitchell Area Historical Society. The author is especially indebted to James D. Hopkins, the bank's president, and to the society's committee for the project—Lyle W. Swenson, James C. Hunt and Clyde Goin—who not only provided the necessary assistance but made the work enjoyable.

Much of the research was done at the Mitchell Public Library where librarian Jackie Traut was most cooperative. As they have in the past, the librarians of the Yankton Community Library provided inter-library loan materials and responded to other information requests cheerfully and efficiently. The same was true of Laura Glum and the staff members of the South Dakota State Historical Society research center in Pierre and the Layne Library at Dakota Wesleyan University. Similarly, the resources of the Friends of the Middle Border Museum were made readily available by curator Hazel Jordan and her successor, Gwenna Henricks.

James D. McLaird, professor of history at D.W.U., helped tremendously by filling in some important blank spots when it was most needed, while Pat Helgeland of the Mitchell Chamber of Commerce merits an extra thank-you for multiple reasons. There were many others, too, who contributed to the final product in one way or another: William and Alice Timmins, Pat Amert of the Oscar Howe Art Center, Mary Goin, Garvin Bertsch, Bob Brooks, Charles "Chuck" Rozum, Wally Scott, Tony and Devonia Oster, Billie and Wally Zeal, Marvin L. Stavig for photographic supplies, Debra Kuchera, Hazel Smith, Al Dowling, Gloria Cofer Hanson for her "Remember When" series in *The Daily Republic,* Irma Helgeland, Jeff Logan, the Davison County sheriff's office staff, Charlotte "Charlie" Bruning, Karen Jorgenson, Kelly Hertz, Diane Lehman, Dr. Richard I. Porter and those who contributed photos (not all of which could be used). To any others who may have been inadvertently overlooked, gratitude is no less sincere and apologies are extended.

Appreciation to Clyde Goin must be reiterated for the countless hours he spent in the darkroom copying pictures and for his ceaseless devotion to the endeavor. And once again—for almost more times than I can remember—I could never have met the publisher's deadline without the supporting efforts of my wife Phyllis, my partner and prodder. If the book is a success, they all deserve hearty applause. The author will assume the responsibility for any shortcomings.

—*B.K.*

(Opposite page) Davison County National Guard troops served on the Mexican border, and shortly after their return home were called up again for World War I duty. In 1917 Governor Peter Norbeck spoke in the Corn Palace at a civic gathering in honor of the soldiers seen in the crowd at the governor's left. Mitchell Area Historical Society/L. E. Stair photo.

Palaces Of The Past
First introduced in Mitchell in 1892, the "world's only Corn Palace" was still going strong in the third of three buildings more than a hundred years later. Except for a hiatus from 1894 through 1899, plus one year in a tent, the annual harvest festival has survived through wars, depressions, fickle weather and fiscal uncertainty. A more detailed history follows in Chapter 5.

The Corn-Palace

MITCHELL CORN-PALACE

MITCHELL CORN PALACE

CHAPTER 1

It All Began at Firesteel

Heman Cady Greene, a surveyor and native of Stratford, New York, seemed to have that nagging spirit of restlessness which characterized so many men lured by the Western frontier. He, along with his wife's bachelor brother, John Head, had already been involved in the early development of Rochester, Minnesota; but, for them, the quest for greener pastures still called them elsewhere: this time to the relatively unpopulated plainsland of Dakota Territory.

In 1870 the two men—along with Greene's wife, their two children and several other families—left Minnesota in three prairie schooners and eventually relocated in the village of Bon Homme near the Missouri River. There Heman acquired government surveying contracts and served for a time as secretary to the territorial council at the capital in Yankton.

One of his contracts took him up the James River in 1871 where he came upon a tract of land near the mouth of a small stream which the Sioux Indians called *Chanka Wakpan*. White explorers referred to it as Firesteel Creek, so called because of the flintstone found along its banks. Incidentally, that portion of the Dakota Territory had been visited in 1855 by an expedition of U. S. Topographical Engineers led by Lt. Gouveneur Kemble Warren who later wrote in his report that the land west of the 97th meridian was not fit for agricultural settlement and that it should be "occupied by a pastoral people, whether civilized or savage."

(Opposite page) The valley of Firesteel Creek (beyond the curve at right) was the scene of Davison County's first settlement. However, the area was subject to flooding, so the village was abandoned, and Mitchell was established on the higher ground to the west. Mitchell Area Historical Society.

Despite Warren's assessment of the region, the Firesteel Creek location appealed to Greene and John Head who had accompanied him on the surveying expedition. They both filed pre-emption claims at the land office in Vermillion; and H. C.'s dugout, burrowed into the creek bluff, is said to be the first habitation by a white person in what was to become Davison County. A year later he had lumber hauled from Yankton and built a frame house into which he moved his wife Frances, daughter Louise and son Theodore.

As other equally optimistic homesteaders arrived in the area, the Greenes' home became the gathering spot for a developing community called Firesteel (often, in the beginning, spelled as two words). The embryonic village—which originally was intended to be named Minneota—was strategically located on one of the trails to Fort Thompson on the Missouri. Later a stage line brought pas-

Davison County had its beginnings in the village of Firesteel which was also the first county seat. This historic photo, dated 1879, includes the area's earliest pioneer merchants and professional men, most of whom relocated in Mitchell when the railroad bypassed Firesteel. Mitchell Area Historical Society/Lavilla D. Hammer collection.

sengers from Bon Homme, Springfield and Yankton on a route known as the Jimtown Trail which eventually extended northward through Forestburg to Jamestown.

Already at that early time there was great interest in railroad expansion among opportunistic territorial politicians. In 1872—even before the first Dakota Southern train arrived in Yankton from Sioux City or before there were sufficient voters in the region north of the earlier settlements—the territorial legislature designated six long, narrow unorganized counties with speculative dreams of extended rail lines and greater populations in what became known as the county-creating orgy of 1873. The boundaries of existing Hutchinson and Hanson counties were revised, and Armstrong, Bramble, Miner and Davison were added.

The latter took its name from Maine native Henry Caleb Davison who came to Bon Homme County in 1869 with his wife Alberta. Son of a ship's captain who lost his life at sea, Davison—with his brother-in-law, George Mead—operated general stores in Bon Homme, Springfield and at Choteau Creek, selling—among other merchandise—groceries, cigars and liquor. Despite its early successes, the firm apparently failed, and Davison took over the International Hotel in Springfield which he operated for several years. For a time he served as postmaster at Bon Homme and was chairman of the county Democratic central committee, attending the national convention in Baltimore in 1872. Although he lost an election bid for county coroner, he no doubt made enough friends among territorial politicians—possibly because of his liquor business—to have a county named in his honor.

Although he never became a resident of the county bearing his name, Davison bought and leased land northwest of Firesteel where he was involved in cattle raising with several partners. However, his various enterprises suffered financial reverses, and it was reported that he and his associates lost cattle in a blizzard. *The Mitchell Capital* of September 18, 1879, revealed that he, William P. Dewey, A. H. Barnes and George W. Kingsbury owed $26.40 in delinquent taxes on 140 acres of Davison County land for the years 1876, 1877 and 1878. Davison's political connections were evident in that two of his partners—Kingsbury, the prominent Yankton newspaper publisher, and Dewey, the territorial surveyor-general from 1873 to 1877—each had counties named for them, too.

In addition to business failures, cattle losses and back taxes, Davison also had other problems. His wife divorced him on July 4, 1878, charging cruelty; and on September 14, 1880, he was the subject of an insanity petition filed in Bon Homme County. When he died ten days later in Springfield—two months before his 39th birthday—his obituary stated: "Mr. Davison has suffered with mental derangement which grew upon him until about a year ago he became perfectly helpless and in which sad state he remained until his death ended his sufferings." According to the *Springfield Times*, he died in the home of his "aged mother who has cared for him with the most tender devotion." No mention was made of his connection with Davison County, his two children or of his ex-wife who later married George W. Snow, a former salesman and bookkeeper for H. C. Davison & Company during its heyday.

In 1874 Davison County was officially organized, with Firesteel as the county seat, although there were scarcely enough adult male residents to vote and to fill the various governmental positions. Women, sad to say, were denied the ballot in those days. Commissioners John Head, Levi Hain and Joseph Platt were initially appointed by Governor John J. Pennington. Then, with less than two dozen voters casting ballots at the Greene house in the fall of 1874, Luke W. Lowell, R. P. Cady and Head became the first elected commissioners. Other officers were filled by appointment; and—

In the pioneering days, itinerant bands of Indians camped occasionally along Firesteel Creek in the Mitchell area, but contacts between the nomadic Sioux and the settlers were generally friendly and without confrontation. Mitchell Area Historical Society/L. E. Stair photo.

apparently for lack of available candidates—John Morris, who became an Episcopalian minister, was named county treasurer, judge of probate and superintendent of schools.

Geographically, the original Davison County was not at all like its final shape. It was approximately 12 miles from north to south and 36 miles east and west, with Firesteel almost at the western end and extending eastward over what was generally the northern half of later-day Hanson and Miner counties.

Brothers Heman C. (standing) and Israel Greene (seated, opposite page) were two of the principal founders of Davison County, arriving in the Firesteel area before the county was organized and being involved in much of the early surveying work. Mitchell Area Historical Society.

There was very little governmental business in those first years, and pioneer liveryman Curtis Ambrose recalled that the original county records—kept on a tablet of foolscap paper, probably by Sheriff Rufus F. Alterton—were blown away by a tornado which destroyed Alterton's claim shack. The mid-1870s also brought grasshoppers, blizzards and floods, so development was slow. Much of the activity, social and otherwise, centered around the Greene house. It served as a temporary hotel for new homesteaders until they could provide their own shelter; and years later in her memoirs, Louise Greene Hammer recalled:

"When court was necessary, our dining room became a court house. When missionaries were on their circuit, our parlor became a chapel. Our house was named the post office with Uncle John Head as post master and father as mail carrier, on horseback, between Springfield and our home. Mother's precious bureau felt the gavel, the sorting of mail, the chalice of the chapel . . . Because of the good floor, dances were held at our home [too]."

Louise also remembered a three-day springtime blizzard when four adult Indians and five children were marooned with them in their home. Of immediate concern were a half dozen new calves in the barn. While one of the Indian men stood in the doorway shouting loudly and incessantly so they wouldn't lose their way, John Head and two other Indians struggled back and forth through the snow until the calves were safely in the house. Unfortunately, when the storm abated and the men tunneled through the drifts to the barn, they found eleven head of cattle frozen to death. The Indians helped butcher the animals and received meat and hides for their work. They also gathered ducks and geese caught by a quick freeze in the creek and river. Louise helped her mother dress the waterfowl, and her father took them on his mail route, trading them for supplies along the way.

Indians did not seem to be a particular concern for the white settlers although there were occasional incidents, mostly involved with demands for food by small groups of transients. However, there still was an underlying wariness which was evident in another of Louise's recollections:

"In 1871 . . . I experienced my greatest fright. Prairie fire. The whole town turned out with sacks, pails and brooms. Soon a man came running to our house and said that the Indians had set the fire and were coming to massacre everyone. Then Uncle Charley (Baker) came to get all the firearms we had. He took all but father's shotgun. Mother began packing her keepsakes and food. I was shaking so with fear that I could not even stand. Night had come and there was a bright moon. I would crawl from one bed to another asking whether the Indians were near. But they did not come, nor had they set the fire."

Also among the earliest inhabitants of the Firesteel area was Major Israel Greene and his wife Edmonia. His military rank was a carry-over from the Civil War when he served in the Confederate Marine Corps. Earlier, however, H. C. Greene's brother had been a lieutenant in the U. S. Marines, accompanying Commodore Matthew C. Perry on his precedent-setting visit to Japan in 1853, studying artillery science at West Point and playing a key role in a noteworthy episode in American history. It was Lieutenant Greene who led the assault on the Harper's Ferry Arsenal which resulted in the capture and eventual hanging of the rebellious abolitionist John Brown. To Israel's misfortune, history gives most of the credit for the raid to Lt. Col. Robert E. Lee, who, in civilian clothes, was called in to direct the operation from a distance. However, Lee's official report at least noted that the leader of the insurgents, John Brown, "was cut down by the sword of Lieutenant Greene."

Ironically, both Lee and Greene—the latter a descendant of

General Nathaniel Greene of Revolutionary War fame—switched over to the Confederate forces when the Civil War began. Although he was Northern-born, Israel Greene had married the daughter of a Virginia planter whose people were friends and neighbors of the Lees. Because of this, he opted to align himself with the rebel cause. After the war his Confederate service apparently became known to Minnesota Unionists and may have been a factor in his brother's move to Dakota. After he also filed a claim in the Firesteel area, Major Greene became involved with Heman in various surveying projects. Meanwhile, his wife Edmonia established a school in their home, thus beginning the county's long educational heritage.

As more and more homesteaders arrived in the region, the village of Firesteel grew correspondingly. In the spring of 1876—when the rest of the nation was celebrating its centennial, and shortly before Lt. Col. George Armstrong Custer and men of his Seventh Cavalry were annihilated at Little Big Horn—Cyrus B. Ingham began publishing his *Jim River Advocate,* taking advantage of the required land-notice advertising to finance his short-lived newspaper. It was said that Ingham's press already had played a great role in American journalistic history, having been rescued from the Mississippi River where it had been thrown by a mob after Elijah P. Lovejoy, the editor, was murdered defending it and his abolitionist paper at Alton, Illinois, in 1837. *The Advocate* appeared intermittently for about 18 months, but Ingham finally gave up and moved back to Beloit, Wisconsin.

The defunct paper was then succeeded by the *Firesteel Mail* published by John W. Walsh. In the meantime, William Van Eps had opened a general store, Carl Eilers a tinshop, S. Norton became the town smithy and in time Firesteel could boast 32 motley buildings of varying shapes and sizes between the river and the creek.

This was the era when being in the vanguard of railroad expansion had the potential for sudden wealth. At the same time it was a giant guessing game as to future track locations and the creation of new towns. By 1879 the Chicago, Milwaukee & St. Paul Railroad Company had reached Marion Junction from its entry into Dakota Territory at Canton. The next hurdle on the route to the Missouri was the Jim River, and the citizens of Firesteel and rival Rockport on the stage line some 11 miles to the south were equally hopeful that they would be the beneficiaries of the crossing. They were both wrong.

At Firesteel a railroad surveyor supposedly saw a piece of driftwood either lodged in a tree or lying on high ground along the creek. According to local legend, that was indication to him that the village was in a flood plain and therefore not suitable for permanent development. However, evidence of the railway company's plans should have become obvious on May 5, 1879, when John D. Lawler, son of a wealthy bridge builder and Milwaukee Road stockholder, bought approximately 75 acres some two miles west of Firesteel. Undoubtedly he had "inside information" because his land just happened to encompass much of the site of a new town to be named in honor of Alexander Mitchell, Scotland-born president of the C.,M.&St.P. and business associate of the younger Lawler's father.

German immigrant Fritz Peters rented this typical early-day Davison County farm in Baker Township. Pioneer settlers transformed the open prairie into productive land, despite crude beginnings and the ravages of nature. Wenton Peters collection.

LUNCH ROOM
Merchant
TAILOR.

CHAPTER 2

Mitchell: A Prairie Boom Town

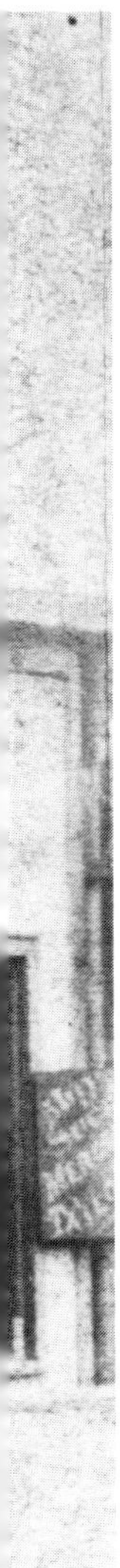

The village of Mitchell got off to what seemed like a promising start in the summer of 1879 even before the railroad arrived. According to old records, Myron H. Rowley platted the townsite and Israel Greene later surveyed it, each for a reported fee of 10 dollars. By then the exodus from Firesteel had begun. One of the earliest arrivals was David A. Mizener, a young lawyer who opened the first real estate office in Mitchell. He shared a 12x16 shack with John Walsh and his printing press. The latter wanted to get the jump on other publishers sure to be lured by the development. His new paper was named *The Capital*, and on September 18, 1879, in his first issue, the enterprising journalist announced:

"Our action in transferring our office from Firesteel to Mitchell at so early a date in the history of the latter seems to be regarded as somewhat premature by some of our friends . . . It has always been our idea that wherever the Milwaukee Company located their depot at the crossing of the Jim River, there would be a good town . . . therefore Mitchell is the point for us. We moved thus early . . . and we are none too soon as lots are being sold very fast . . . and it will not be long before the whistle of the locomotive will be sounding in our ears."

Walsh added that "the hammer, saw and plane make inspiring music in Mitchell these days." Joining the rush to the new location were storekeeper William Van Eps, carpenter William A. Cox, pharmacist brothers Frank and Alson Hammer and other eager opportunists, many of whom towed their ramshackle buildings with them behind horses and oxen. Jacob K. Smith came from Firesteel and sold bacon and flour from a covered wagon before his grocery store was built.

(Opposite page) Samuel Webber was one of Mitchell's earliest settlers and restaurant operators. As early as 1883 he reputedly served oysters "second to no place in the West." Later he was one of the founders of the Commercial Savings Bank. Mitchell Area Historical Society.

In the spring of 1880 the river was bridged and the tracks laid into Mitchell, but even before the first passenger train arrived on May 16, Frederic E. Moses brought two wagon loads of lumber from the temporary terminus at Alexandria. Neither he nor other suppliers could keep up with the demand as boarding houses, a livery stable, hotels and other rudimentary business places were established almost immediately. Then came the first setback.

A tornado struck the new town in May, and Fred Moses described the destruction:

"The air was filled with dirt and sticks which beat against my

(Top) Laying railroad tracks across the Dakota prairie was relatively uncomplicated until streams like the Jim River required bridging. The construction from Mitchell to Arlandton and beyond proceeded rapidly with few geographic barriers. Mount Vernon Library.

(Bottom) Building Davison County's railroad trestles with horse-drawn equipment was a slow, tedious process. The Jim River, Firesteel Creek and other small streams had to be bridged for both the Milwaukee and Omaha lines. Mitchell Area Historical Society.

office. The darkness thickened . . . I saw a roof taken off the building across the street . . . every building on the south side of First Avenue was either moved or damaged. Stables were blown away, leaving horses tied to their mangers . . . Men on Main Street were running to Arneson's saloon, a building made of chalkstone masoned with mud as no lime was available in '79. The roof was taken off. The walls fell in, killing two men. The saloon was filled to capacity with men who thought they would be safe, which shows that a saloon . . . never was a safe place for men at any time."

Another pioneer in his reminiscences recalled that it was Jacob Luther and Henry S. Smith who lost their lives and that the Foley and Devy saloon and billiard hall was the scene of the tragedy. Whatever the case, after the storm the building boom continued. Stewart F. Goodykoontz established his Mitchell Exchange Bank. Lawrence O. Gale, who had operated a hotel in Rockport, cut his building in half and moved it to Mitchell. The drugstore he eventually established featured jewelry, books, stationery, wallpaper and paint as well as the needs of a growing number of doctors. A brickyard with six kilns worked overtime to keep up with the construction.

In the meantime, an election had been held on the previous November 4th, and Mitchell had wrested the county seat from Firesteel by a vote of 112 to 30. Then in September of 1880 a U. S. Land Office serving ten counties east of the Missouri River was assigned to the new town. Thus Mitchell became the region's focal point for prospective homesteaders, 200 of whom made entries on the first day of business. It quickly became a marketplace as well. A rosy future seemed assured, but the incessant development was interrupted by another unexpected calamity.

On October 15—when farmers were in the midst of harvesting, and winter preparations had not yet been made—an unseasonal

blizzard struck and continued unabated for three days and nights, with fierce winds driving the powdery snow which pioneers described as being "fine as flour." It was the beginning of the historic "long winter" of 1880-81 which ravaged the entire Dakota Territory and was immortalized by novelist Laura Ingalls Wilder.

As they did elsewhere across the stricken prairie, settlers in Mitchell and the surrounding area ran dangerously short of food, coal and kerosene. Railroad ties, telegraph poles and bridge materials meant for further extension of the line were used to keep homes warm. According to one pioneer's recollections, the Milwaukee Road made every other tie under the rails available for fuel at a cost of 35 cents each, but he said that they burned so poorly in his coal stove that he got warmer cutting them up than burning them. Those who couldn't get wood made do with "prairie coal" as twisted hay was called.

Coffee mills were used to grind flour and corn meal, while dwindling supplies of sugar, coffee, tea and other staples were shared. John Walsh's paper had been joined by the *Mitchell Gazette* in the competition for land-notice advertising, and when newsprint supplies ran short, the publishers printed on wrapping paper, wallpaper and even cotton cloth. Livestock wandered away and froze. Wildlife suffered severely, especially antelope, still quite common in the region and which provided a supply of tough, stringy meat which the settlers boiled with vegetables to make it palatable. Many antelope were reported killed by wolves and coyotes when their hooves broke through the crusted snow while their pursuers ran safely over the packed surface.

The intermittent blizzards—which piled snow to the depth of from 10 to 12 feet—didn't let up until April, and then the thawing began. The Jim River became a raging torrent from bluff to bluff as the usually docile stream rose to more than 20 feet above its normal level. The wagon and railroad bridges to Mitchell were washed away and the fledgling town was isolated from its source of supply to the east. On one occasion the Greene brothers along with Rufus Alterton, the county's first elected sheriff, volunteered to row across the swollen stream for desperately needed provisions. With Alterton at the oars and H. C. Greene at the rudder, Major Greene battled floating trees and islands of brush from his position at the bow. In time the crossing was made and a load of flour taken on, but on the return trip much of the precious cargo had to be thrown out to keep the boat from being swamped.

Fortunately, no human lives were lost, and when the crisis passed, the building of Mitchell—incorporated in 1881 as a village—was renewed with increased fervor. The first board of trustees—consisting of James D. Devy, James S. Foster, P. T. McGovern, Joseph L. Davenport, Arad J. LaBarre and E. W. Taylor — met on May 7 that

Homesteading in Davison County pitted land-seeking settlers against nature on the relatively barren Dakota plains. They came by horse, oxen, railroad and afoot, and their first habitations were often sod houses or dugouts. Mitchell Area Historical Society.

Though the water was hard and had considerable mineral content, flowing artesian wells were a great boon to Davison County farmers, not only for household use but for thirsty livestock on the otherwise dry prairie. J. Leonard Jennewein photo collection with the N. J. Dunham manuscript, Layne Library, Dakota Wesleyan University.

year to begin the process of providing the facilities and services the citizens demanded. Oddly enough, one of their first accomplishments was to establish a pesthouse to confine victims of smallpox and other contagious diseases. After that, further developments literally mushroomed into existence.

Eight gas street lamps were installed on Main Street, and John O. Walrath—who later became a prominent banker—was paid $34 a month as the village lamplighter. Ordinances were passed to prohibit filling street ruts with manure; that all dead animals had to be buried instead of being piled up at the edge of town; and hay stacks within the village had to be 100 feet from any building. Wooden sidewalks of two-inch planks were built so the ladies' long dresses wouldn't drag in the dust and mud.

During the first several years of the 1880s, construction was rampant. By 1883 the population reached 1,000, and it doubled in the following year. Mitchell officially became a town with Dr. Chauncey S. Burr as the first mayor. It boasted seven hotels, four barber shops, 23 law offices, seven general stores, three drugstores, three newspapers, six millinery shops and several dozen other assorted businesses. One of the four banks was founded by brothers W. George and Nathan L. Davison (no known relation to the man after whom the county was named) and eventually became the First Mitchell National Bank. There were seven churches to offset to some degree the nine saloons.

With an active Board of Trade sending out glowing descriptions of the town and county, the phenomenal growth continued. Corresponding secretary of the board was lawyer James S. Foster, a master promoter who, some 20 years earlier, had a similar position with the Free Homestead Association of Syracuse, New York, and was largely responsible for luring the so-called New York Colony to Dakota Territory. Augmented by the strategic location of the land office and the sales pitches of the railroad company, the Board of Trade offered various inducements to bring merchants, manufacturers, churchmen and educators to Mitchell. Foster, in addition to his business as a land agent, also edited the *Dakota Advocate*, a real estate and immigration paper of which some 100,000 copies reportedly had been sent back East and to Europe.

While it is impossible—without creating an encyclopedic tome — to include all of the early developments, a sampling will indicate the scope of activity. By 1884—when the town had some 4,000 residents—manager William Layton of the Erie Telephone and Telegraph Company had more than 50 crude phones in operation just eight years after Alexander Graham Bell unveiled his first experimental model. However, the venture soon proved unprofitable and the phones were collected up and moved to Sioux Falls. The *Mitchell Capital* breathed an editorial sigh and commented: "thus the city is relieved of another nuisance."

Cultural activities were not overlooked, and citizens raised $600 to provide "magnificent uniforms" for a 14-piece cornet band. A daily stage carried mail to Yankton and Huron, with semi-weekly runs to Springfield and Wessington Springs. There was a virtual litany of land brokers, money-lenders and lawyers on the scene, along with at least eight medical doctors, two dentists and Dr. M. Halfhide, an optician and oculist who advertised "two weeks' treatment free of charge in all chronic cases and satisfaction guaranteed or no charge." He was credited with "miraculously restoring the sight of two area homesteaders."

An artificial stone works provided building material for a new courthouse and the offices of the *Republican*, one of four newspapers in town, plus Foster's *Dakota Advocate*. James Leslie opened a boot and shoe manufactory on Main Street; and to supplement that business, he sold walnut, butternut and ash tree seeds, as well as cuttings and saplings of cottonwood, boxelder, soft maple, evergreens and fruit trees, all needed by tree claim developers.

(Top) As president of the Milwaukee Road, Scotland-born Alexander Mitchell was largely responsible for the railway's expansion into Dakota Territory where it had 1,215.11 miles of track at the time of his death on April 19, 1887. The Corn Palace City was named in his honor. Friends of the Middle Border Museum.

(Bottom) Railroad passengers were brought from the railroad depot to the Alexander Mitchell and other hotels by horse-drawn hack, the taxi cabs of the day. Mitchell Area Historical Society.

According to a promotion booklet, R. F. Krueger embarked on the "manufacture of all summer drinks, such as champagne, cider, ginger ale, soda, seltzer and mineral waters." The same publication announced that Louis Herzog "flatters himself that he is competent to treat and shoe any horse so as to improve him, if it is within the power of any smith to do it." Herzog also made the iron grates for the doors of the town jail. It was said that no one ever escaped through the grates; they went through the roof. On Main Street W. C. Kratz made and sold cigars with such brand names as Belle of Mitchell, Fountain City, W.C.K. and Acme; and Samuel Webber's restaurant reputedly served oysters "second to no place in the West."

The three-story Alexander Mitchell House operated by Colonel Joseph L. Davenport, former purveyor to the Indians, was touted as the "finest hotel in Dakota," complete with reading rooms, sample rooms for commercial men and a dining room with a seating capacity of 350. Supposedly, the railroad brought in Davenport's construction supplies free of charge, so he named his hostelry after the company's president. Livery stables, harness shops, a bath house, hardware and implement stores, at least one billiard parlor and Abe W. O'Dell's ice company (capable of storing 500 tons of ice "harvested from the pure waters of Firesteel Creek") all added to the business activity of the burgeoning town.

Unfortunately, the boom period didn't last. Except for scattered unproductive tracts, the available homestead land had been taken up and most "ground floor" entreprenurial opportunities had waned. Crop prices dropped, and shipping charges on the railroads began to work to the detriment of farmers. Worst of all, however, the weather turned bad. A series of drouth years beginning in 1886, further complicated by severe winters, took the bloom off the early enthusiasm of many settlers. Those who were heavily indebted couldn't pay their mortgages and other bills. Not too few simply packed up and headed back East.

The greatest calamity struck on Thursday, the 12th of January, 1888. The particular day dawned balmy and pleasant despite the midwinter date. Children had trudged off to rural schools; farmers in shirtsleeves had driven to market or were away from home doing seasonal chores. Suddenly the mild southeast breezes brought a shower of rain, and then without warning, the wind switched to the northwest, the temperature plummeted and the rain turned to sleet and granular snow. For more than a dozen hours the blizzard raged across the Territory. Men were trapped in the fields; livestock wandered

Before horse-drawn fire wagons, the Mitchell firefighters towed their hose-and-bucket cart by rope, practicing for coordination and speed. Members of the volunteer company posed before the chalkstone Hammer and Hammer Drug Store at First and Main. The Hammer brothers, Frank and Alson, established their business in 1879 before the railroad arrived. Mitchell Area Historical Society.

This is how Mitchell looked to a traveling artist in 1883. The view is from south to north, with the new courthouse dominant on the horizon. The estimated population that year was 1,000. Mitchell Area Historical Society.

aimlessly until they became stranded in drifts to freeze; but saddest of all, many youngsters were released by their teachers when the weather began to change and before they could get home, they were engulfed by what became known as the "children's blizzard."

In Davison County Miss Bertha Smith, the teacher in Baker No. 4, became an unsung heroine as she placed her back against the schoolhouse door and defied her students—some of them husky farm boys more than 16 years old—who wanted to go home through the storm. Undoubtedly she saved their lives. During the night the fuel ran out, so she tied scarves and ropes together so the outdoor coal bin could be reached without anyone being lost.

On Friday the 13th, survivors throughout Dakota emerged from their places of safety to search for those who were not so lucky. When the gruesome figures were tallied, it was revealed that the storm had left at least 112 dead in the southern half of the Territory, with Bon Homme County losing 19, Beadle 18, Hutchinson 15, and fortunately enough, Davison only one. The latter was 13-year-old Arthur Allen who died after he and his father had been caught in the blizzard while they were attempting to bring in a load of hay. They spent the night in a cave dug into a snow bank on the Firesteel north of Mitchell. Although they tried desperately to stay warm by constant movement, the boy perished from exhaustion and exposure by early morning.

In Mitchell Thomas Ball and a neighbor gathered up all the clotheslines they could find and tied them together to make guide ropes to reach Whittier School where they brought comforters, a lantern and sacks of food for Ball's daughter Nellie and other children marooned there with the janitor and their teacher, Miss Nellie Nelings. She put benches together to make beds, while the janitor managed to bring in enough coal to keep the stove going throughout

The Mitchell Iron and Supply Company was founded by George H. Summers in 1884 under the name of the Mitchell Iron and Boiler Works and eventually became the oldest family owned and operated business in the county. While Summers and his men worked on massive equipment of the era—like the Avery steam tractor (right)—he was equally proud of his floral garden alongside the plant which he personally tended and shared with young and old (above). Darwin F. and Charles H. Summers collection.

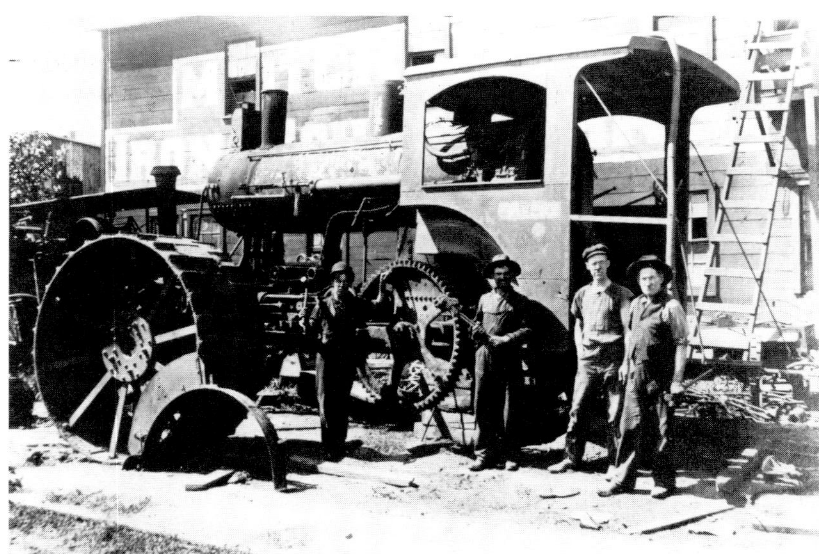

the night. For them it was a reasonably comfortable adventure.

Elsewhere in the county, others were not so lucky. Lena Bruhn went to search for her husband Hans who had not returned from the barn. Becoming disoriented, she wandered until she reached the wash shanty of a neighbor south of Mount Vernon. Although she could hear someone ringing a dinner bell from the house not far away, she chose not to attempt to reach it. In the subzero weather, both her feet were frozen and parts of them had to be amputated.

A similar loss of limbs was suffered by Kate Dodd, the organist of the Methodist Church in Ethan. She and her husband Asa and six-year old niece had tried to reach home after visiting a neighbor, but their horses became confused and wandered around until exhausted. Asa Dodd then wrapped his wife and niece in his coat and left them with the wagon while he tried to find his house. So typically in the blinding snow, he, too, lost his way until he stumbled onto the home of Swan Rosenquist some two miles away. The two of them then searched till dark for the woman and child with no success. Finally, in the early morning they found them. Mrs. Dodd's feet were frozen, but the young girl eventually recovered without lasting effects.

To illustrate how legends are born, another version of this episode reported that the child was the Dodds' daughter Nellie, the wagon was an overturned sleigh, Asa searched with an unknown stranger and the family dog huddled with the two survivors, helping to keep them warm. Regardless of the conflicting details, one fact is certain: Kate Dodd suffered the amputations, and the centennial history of Ethan's United Methodist Church recorded that "she continued to play for services, even under extreme pain."

In the aftermath of the storm, the challenging weather and unfavorable economic conditions continued. Then, in 1889—as Davison County and Mitchell, the county seat, struggled through the ups and downs of their first decade—South Dakota became a state, and a new era was about to begin.

This undated parade photo offers an historic view of Mitchell's Main Street and Second Avenue. The streets were still unpaved, but electric power and phone lines had been installed. Mitchell Area Historical Society.

CHAPTER 3

Land as Rich as the Valley of the Nile

Backing up a bit, when the territorial legislature met in 1881, two bills were introduced to redefine the boundaries of earlier hastily created counties. As a result, the residents of Hanson and Davison were faced with two choices.

The first was to combine the two, retaining only the Hanson name. The second was to split them down the middle, after adding four townships on the west, creating, in effect, twin counties of 12 townships each. These propositions were then submitted to a vote of the people who rejected the former and approved the latter. The results were especially influenced by the voters of Mitchell and Alexandria, both county seats and one of which would lose the political plum if a single county was formed.

While the earliest development centered around Firesteel and Mitchell, settlement throughout the surrounding area was spurred by the expected railroad expansion and the activities of the land boomers. The latter were effusive—if not imaginative—in the promotion of Davison and adjoining counties.

One promotion booklet published in 1883 for prospective homesteaders in the East described the Jim River valley as "equal in richness and productiveness to that of the River Nile." To counter negative assertions of Eastern newspapers about blizzards and summer storms, the bulletin insisted that "South Dakota (not yet a state) has not been visited by a tornado in the memory of the oldest white man." Obviously overlooked was the twister that almost blew Mitchell away in 1880.

A headline bragged: "South Dakota Is the Place for the Poor Man." Then the copy went on to say that the best soil in the world—with the sward easily broken with two horses or one yoke of oxen—could be had for from $4 to $12 an acre. The writer continued to extol the virtues of the region:

"Why do you remain in the old worn-out States, toiling and wearing away your lives? Come to the beautiful prairies of South Dakota, get 160 or 320 acres of land in which is the foundation of wealth and comfort . . . The old States are good enough to be born in, but South Dakota is the place to live in."

To the west of Mitchell, Charles H. Arland had homesteaded along the Fort Thompson Trail in what was then Aurora County.

(Opposite page) Despite tourism, retail trade and manufacturing industries, agriculture has remained the bedrock of Davison County's economy since pioneer days. This early-day harvesting photo was taken in Badger Township near Loomis. Mitchell Area Historical Society.

(Top) Mount Vernon was first known as Arlandton when the Milwaukee Road extended its tracks westward from Mitchell in 1881. Harve Dwight was listed as the first depot agent. Wally Scott collection.

(Bottom) Evan D. Watkins was an early convert to mechanized farming in Davison County when he bought a Hart-Parr Oil Tractor and gang plow in 1912. He and his son Ben were featured in the company's advertising booklet titled "How Two Farmers Succeed." Maxine Johnson collection.

Like the Greenes' residence at Firesteel, his home became a stopping place for travelers, and in time a village grew up around it. Arlandton, as it was called, appeared on survey maps as early as 1879. Two years later, when the railroad pushed westward, there were 13 voters in the embryonic town which was located adjacent to the new tracks. Unfortunately for the Arlands, their family name eventually disappeared from the map, supposedly when postal officials decided that Arlandton would be confused with the postoffice of Arlington in Kingsbury County. However, that may be one of those continuing historical errors because Arlington was known as Nordland at the time.

Just who originally applied the name Mount Vernon to the former Arlandton has never been established, although it may have been a Virginian or someone who had memories of George Washington's estate. The town plat was recorded in 1882 about the same time that John Pease established *The Mt. Vernon Gazette*. By the following year a hardware store, livery stable, lumber yard, drugstore, cigar manufactory, postmaster Charles Arland's hotel and several other firms were in business. A two-story school house was also built so that teachers Jessie Braught and Lucy Burns could begin classes in January of 1883.

Like Mitchell, Mount Vernon had an exuberant beginning, but in the latter half of the 1880s the boom fizzled and growth slowed to a virtual halt because of drouth, grasshoppers and poor farm prices, a triumvirate of miseries which was to visit South Dakota periodically through the years. The town survived the infamous blizzard of '88, although fuel and food were in short supply, and at least one edition of *The Mt. Vernon Gazette* appeared on pink sale-bill paper.

In 1889 when the southern half of Dakota Territory achieved statehood, Mount Vernon suffered its most serious setback. On April 3 that year, local citizens were alarmed to see a heavy band of smoke being driven toward the town from the northwest by a 50-mile-an-hour wind. Tinder dry prairie grass fed the flames which roared southeastward across the plains. There was no way to stem the fury, and when it finally burned itself out—with the help of firefighters who came from Mitchell on a special train—53 buildings in Mount Vernon had been destroyed. The disastrous event would be remembered as one of the most destructive fires in state history.

But the Mount Vernonites quickly proved their tenacity. Although the new state of South Dakota was the victim of a searing drouth and Governor Arthur C. Mellette traveled to Chicago and other major cities to appeal for relief supplies, residents of the burned-out town began the rebuilding process. Even while the remains of his store were still smoldering, James Corey rented another unscathed building and went to Mitchell to secure a new stock of goods. James Haynes, who had come to the region in a horse and buggy with Charles Arland, hurriedly ordered a shipment of lumber. Mary Dougherty, daughter of Postmaster Michael Dougherty, became a local heroine when she saved postal records by stuffing them in a mail pouch and burying it along the railroad tracks. Not so fortunate was *The Mt. Vernon Gazette*, as indicated in a small-sheet edition which editor Edward S. Johnston managed to get printed:

"The books and subscription list of the *Gazette* were all lost in the fire. Any subscriber who fails to receive the paper will understand why, and will kindly send in his name. It is impossible to remake the list without error and some time will be necessary to have it correct."

Johnston did not persist, however, and moved to Mitchell where

Fred Widmann, a German immigrant, came to Davison County in 1882 and established a successful liquor dealership. Henry Clay sour mash whiskey was one of his featured products. He also had a dance hall, a bowling alley and a summer garden in the rear of his store on Mitchell's Main Street. Mitchell Area Historical Society.

The Mt. Vernon Gazette.

VOL. VIII. Mt. Vernon, Dakota, Thursday, April 4, 1889. NO. 5.

THE MT. VERNON GAZETTE

E. S. JOHNSTON, Ed. and Pro.

Subscription, per year in advance, - - $1.50.

Entered at the Mt. Vernon post office as second class matter.

The books and subscription list of the GAZETTE were all lost in the fire. Any subscriber who fails to receive the paper will understand why, and will kindly send in his name. It is impossible to remake the list without error and sometime will be necessary to have it correct.

The Business Portion Of Mt Vernon

Entirely Destroyed By Fire.

One Hundred Families Destitute.

Other Fires of Greater or Less Magnitude.

A DAY OF DIRE DISASTER

The GAZETTE has no apologies to offer for its diminutive size this week. It would probably not have appeared at all, but for the necessity of keeping its legal notices alive. The following account, taken from the Mitchell Republican, while not strictly correct as to the details of the origin of the fire, and the list of losses and insurance, gives an approximate idea of the great calamity that has befallen our fair young town. In the hurry and confusion naturally resulting from the fire we have been unable to prepare an account of the fire and list of those losing, but will give the matter attention next week:

Yesterday was a hard day for the citizens of Mt. Vernon. Seeing the smoke off to the northwest about 11 o'clock they turned out en masse to make a fire break on the north, thinking the west was safe, as it had been burned over in the fall. The fire got the better of them and they worked for nearly two hours in subduing it, and it was during the progress of this fire that they telegraphed to Mitchell for help. Before help came, however, they succeeded in getting it under control, and when the train arrived bearing the Mitchell hook and ladder company and about seventy men they thought there would be little work for them to do. In this, however, they were destined to be most grievously mistaken. Off to the northwest a dense cloud of smoke and dust appeared, but in the terrific gale which was blowing it was impossible to tell whether it was twenty rods or twenty miles away. The Mitchell bucket brigade, however, made a prompt investigation and were meet by dense volumes of flame just outside of the village. Help had arrived not a moment too soon, nor could any advantage have been derived by being upon the ground a moment earlier. For half an hour by vigorous and persistent fighting they kept the fire in subjection, but it was of no use; water was scarce and had to be carried a long distance, and everything was as dry as tinder and the wind blowing at the rate of fifty miles an hour. It was a noble sight to see (if you could but open your eyes to see it)—a hundred men in line, covering a distance not exceeding twenty rods in length right in the midst of the flames and fighting with all the energy of despair. But what was the use! Shavings and cinders and small fragments of boards were carried over the heads of the people a distance of forty—yes, sixty, and perhaps a hundred rods and lodged in hay stacks and around barns and houses, near which by this time was scattered all manner of combustible material. That the head fire must go through the town was now demonstrated beyond the possibility of a doubt, and to limit the width of its scope was now the purpose of everyone. The heat was intense, the smoke was blinding and when the fire got into the buildings the wind seemed to come in terrific guests from every direction. It seemed at one time that there was no possibility of saving anything except the few residences on the south of where the fire first effected an entrance. The flames were driven east from the Methodist church, but by desperate efforts were kept from getting hold of the livery stable belonging to the Mt. Vernon house. They however succeeded in crossing Main street and were driven into the barns belonging to F. D. Powers and George Keeler. On the south side of Second street the first buildings destroyed were the residences owned and occupied by James Corey, Calvin Betts and the hotel and livery stable kept by H. J. Parker. From there east and south nothing is left. All the store buildings, with contents, including the chalk stone bank, together with the depot, elevators and coal warehouses are a mass of ruins. Following is a partial list of the losses with the insurance as near as can be ascertained at present:

	Insurance	Loss
O. McEwan & Son, store building and stock....		$ 6,000
Insured for	$ 2,300	
Parker's drug store......		2,000
Insurance............	500	
Parker's hotel and livery		3,000
No insurance		
F. B. Rich, residence....		700
Insurance.............	300	
Betts, Bras & Co., store building, stock and residence		10,000
Insurance	3,000	
Haynes & Son, lumber and farming implements................		20,000
No insurance		
A. L. Bell, hardware and machinery............		10,000
Insurance............	2,000	

The Mt. Vernon Gazette *was one of the victims of the disastrous fire which destroyed more than 50 buildings in the young town in April of 1889. However, Editor Edward S. Johnston managed to get out a small 8 1/2x11 issue to describe the conflagration and the loss of his subscription list. Mount Vernon Library.*

he published the *Mitchell Gazette* for 18 years. Storekeeper Mark C. Betts and banker Herman H. Garey, who were not driven out by the fire, filled the journalistic void when they started the *Mount Vernon News* in 1893.

Meanwhile, as the main interest was on the east-west railroad development, another line was inching northward from Yankton through Scotland and eventually to Mitchell. It, too, was creating towns along the way. In the southeastern corner of Davison County a small community called Rome had already grown up around Cyrus W. Gillis's store and Ole Rosenquist's blacksmith shop, a postoffice having been established in 1880. As it turned out, Rome suffered a fate similar to that of Firesteel. The railroad passed by to the east, and Ethan—named for the Revolutionary War hero, Ethan Allen—became the surviving town.

Jerome Miles owned most of the land on which the town was originally platted in 1883 in anticipation of the railroad. He built a hotel to accommodate land-seekers and other travelers. Cy Gillis moved his store from Rome, all traces of which eventually disappeared and the land became a cow pasture. A lean-to built on the rear of Gillis's store was used for Ethan's first school, with Nellie King as the teacher.

Like Mitchell and Mount Vernon, the town developed quite rapidly in its first several years. Wooden sidewalks were built on Main Street where a public watering trough and hitching posts were special features. In time carbide street lights were installed. Then the drouth, blizzards and economic woes of the latter half of the 1880s slowed the pace.

The pioneers who stayed on in Davison County during the stressful years which followed were generally a tough, tenacious lot. They survived in dugouts and sod huts, although some had already built sturdy homes of chalkstone and jasper. They buried their diphtheria and cholera-stricken youngsters as well as

(Top) Ethan, like Mitchell and Mount Vernon, was the product of the railroad, and the local depot became the hub of activity for the town. Everything from cream cans to caskets was shipped by train. Leo and Sally Pollreisz collection/Harry B. Hersey photo.

(Bottom) A number of creameries, of varying longevity, were established throughout Davison County. Like the Ethan Creamery Company (shown here), the butter-making plants provided ready cash for area farmers and a skimmed milk by-product for livestock feed. Edwin Blackman was certified as the licensed buttermaker there in 1902. Tony and Devonia Oster collection.

(Top) It was convenient for Ethan visitors and traveling salesmen (then called drummers) to have the Commercial Hotel so close to the railroad depot. Jerome Miles, owner of much of the original townsite, built the first hotel in 1884. J. Leonard Jennewein *photo collection with the* N. J. Dunham *manuscript, Layne Library, Dakota Wesleyan University.*

(Bottom) The dam at White's Mill on the Jim River offered a productive fishing hole for succeeding generations. The mill was built in 1880 and later fell into disrepair. South Dakota Magazine *collection*

their work-worn adults. They watched corn and wheat crops shrivel and die in the sun-baked dust or saw grain and gardens devoured by hordes of grasshoppers. Some were too poor to leave, but mostly it was dogged persistence which held them to the land and struggling towns until things got better.

Each family had its stories of the rigors of those early days. It took Charles Phelps three days to walk from Sioux Falls, wade across the Jim River and then stake his claim east of Ethan. Bostonian R. T. Robinson was too poor to pay stage fare from Yankton, so he, too, walked the 90 miles or so to a homestead in the northeast corner of the county. Men weren't the only land-seekers, though. Miss Kate Anglum came from Iowa to her quarter-section along the Jim River where she broke the sod and dug a well with her own hands. She also had female neighbors in nearby sections of Perry Township where widows Emily Williams and Rhoda Knight established farms on virgin prairie as did Mrs. Sarah Filkins from Pennsylvania who was proud of her 320 acres and the fact that she owned one horse, two oxen, 25 chickens and machinery worth $85.

In his memoirs Dr. Raymond J. Reitzel told how his mother and father came from Illinois and slept under a wagon until they had built a sod house on their claim between Mitchell and Mount Vernon. They had a team of work horses which provided a source of extra cash, being used to help other homesteaders break the land. All was going well until their first child was stricken with diphtheria.

"Father wasted no time mounting Jimbo, his black gelding, and racing 4 1/2 miles to the village of Mount Vernon to which a new doctor had come. The doctor thought it was too stormy to make a night call and sent some medicine for the baby."

"Upon arriving home, Father found that the baby was worse and Mother was distraught. He mounted Florie and this time rode 7 1/2 miles to Mitchell. The doctor there could not come and by the time he returned home, the boy had died. Next morning when the first doctor arrived, Father reached for the buggy whip and chased him off the property."

Despite the hardships, the tenacious pioneers hung on, building, planting and praying for good crops. The county got an important addition as early as 1880 when Thomas Scholfield and his junior partner, John R. White, built a dam and flour mill on the Jim River east of Mitchell. White recalled how settlers came with their grain from miles around, camping overnight to wait for their flour. "We had to run the mill day and night to take care of the business," he said. Ironically, although Scholfield was the experienced miller and eventually bought his partner's interest, the facility became known historically as White's Mill and was a well-known county landmark.

(Top) Chemical Company No. 1 was the pride of the Mitchell Fire Department. Dedicated firefighters were especially important in the era of wooden buildings, heating stoves and early-day electrical wiring. Mitchell Area Historical Society/ Martin K. Eliason photo.

Early-day Mount Vernonites bought shoes, clothing and sundries at the department store founded by Orlando McEwen and continued by his son Elbridge. Wally and Billie Zeal collection.

CHAPTER 4

The Refinement of Churches, Schools and Library Books

In general, the homesteaders in Davison County, as elsewhere in Dakota Territory, tended to be both God-fearing and intensely education-minded. Churches and schools were given high priority in their early building plans.

Episcopalian services were held in the H. C. Greene home at Firesteel by Rev. Melancthon Hoyt of Yankton. Later a sandstone house was converted into a church prior to the arrival of the railroad. Presbyterians had a small chapel in Mitchell when it was first platted in 1879; Baptists apparently used the same building until they had a church of their own.

In 1881 Rev. John R. Reitzel came from the Yale Divinity School to organize a Congregational church, and a year later John Lawler and his wife gave half a city block so an appropriate place of worship could be erected. Lawler also donated land to the Episcopalians so they could move over from Firesteel. At the same time Lutheran missionaries of the Missouri Synod arrived to preach to the German-speaking settlers as well as a growing number of Norwegians. Bishop Martin Marty, the Catholic prelate for the Territory, offered Mass in a Mitchell home in 1880, and shortly afterward the Holy Family parish was organized, according to one unverified story, in a hall over a saloon with planks supported by beer kegs as a substitute for pews. Davison County never had a strongly dominant ethnic group within its population, and the diversity was evident as confessions in the early Mitchell church were heard in English, German and French.

Meanwhile, Methodist missionaries and circuit riders were also active in the area, holding services in various buildings until Reverend Clarence E. Hager completed the first church in the summer of 1883. Similar involvement of various denominations was taking place elsewhere in the county—including the establishment of a Quaker church southwest of Mount Vernon as well as two short-lived Jewish colonies—but the influence of Methodism was especially evident in Mitchell because of a development which was to have a long range impact on the city.

(Opposite page) To qualify teachers for the dozens of rural schools, the Davison County Normal Institute provided the necessary training for certification. Pioneer photographer L. E. Stair captured on film this 1889 class bedecked in the finery of the day. Mitchell Area Historical Society.

Even before the Mitchell church was dedicated, the Dakota Mission Conference of Methodists convened in Parker, and on the agenda was a discussion of the need for an "institution of learning of

Mitchell's ornate Central High School was built in 1895 at a cost of $16,791 on what was known as the Whittier Block. It was later remodeled to serve as the city's junior high for six decades before it was finally razed. Mitchell Area Historical Society.

the higher grade" within the Territory. As a result, three towns—Huron, Ordway and Mitchell—presented proposals to provide a site for the school. Comparisons were made with Mount Vernon, Iowa—home of Cornell, the nearest Methodist college—which was "free from liquor and gambling saloons."

This wasn't the first time Mitchell was in competition with Ordway. The Davison County seat was one of the contenders for the territorial capital, along with Aberdeen, Redfield, Canton, Frankfort, Huron, Steele, Bismarck and Odessa (Devil's Lake). Governor Nehemiah G. Ordway was personally promoting his namesake Brown County town because he just happened to own considerable property there. In the end, the governor's scheme was foiled and Bismarck wrested the prize from Yankton in 1883. Mitchell got one vote from the nine-man selection commission on the 13th and final ballot.

With their capital bid rejected, Mitchellites turned their attention to the college competition. Although the town was still relatively in its infancy, its representatives offered a very generous proposition: 640 acres of land within the city limits, 640 acres adjoining the town, $60,000 in donations and subscriptions and two tracts to be sold for an endowment fund. Ordway's proposition was equally attractive, and again it had the political support of Governor Ordway.

By the time the Methodist leaders met again in Mitchell in October of 1884, the Davison County group already had a basement dug and the walls under construction for a three-story building. When the cornerstone was laid on September 3, a parade formed downtown and an enthusiastic citizenry—including the fire department—marched out to the prospective campus site. Ordway, meanwhile, had only begun excavation. At the conference a heated debate ensued. The Huron bid was rejected, but the other two candidates were in fierce opposition. During the debate an Ordway proponent asked what his town should do with its hole in the ground if it were not selected. According to Oscar W. Coursey's history of Dakota Wesleyan's first fifty years, a Mitchell supporter shouted: "Cut it up in sections and sell it for post holes!"

Some delegates favored a school at both locations, but in the end Mitchell prevailed. Merrill Memorial Hall—named for Bishop S. M. Merrill—was completed in 1885 and classes were begun. However, because of the economic doldrums which followed, Mitchell's ambitious offerings had to be scaled back, and Dakota University—as the new school was called—got underway with somewhat limited means. Though it had only a single building, it quickly became the town's centerpiece of cultural development.

Just two months after the fateful blizzard of January 1888 an even greater tragedy struck Dakota University. At about three a.m. on March 9, a fire of unknown origin engulfed Merrill Hall when there were both students and faculty members sleeping in the building. Before the hall burned to the ground, two young men leaped to their death from the third floor, and several others were severely injured. Professor T. A. Duncan found a clothesline and let himself down from the roof, suffering from lacerated hands and burned feet. Four young ladies threw their bedding out of a second-story window, using it to cushion their fall when they jumped. Luckily they avoided serious injury, but they learned later that they could have walked down to safety because the fire had not yet reached the stairs outside their door.

The Mount Vernon Volunteer Fire Department was organized in 1905 after the town was victimized by two major fires in 1889 and 1904. Note the teddy bear mascot. Mount Vernon Library.

The disaster could well have doomed the school, but the people of Mitchell—not just the Methodists—responded to the crisis by renting the Barber building on Main Street and offering it to the college free of charge. In addition, $8,000 was subscribed for operating expenses; the faculty and Dr. William Bush—the school's first president—accepted the necessary sacrifices; and on September 25, 1888, the fall term opened with 52 students in attendance.

Somehow or other the institution weathered the setback, College Hall was erected on the site of the first building and other facilities added. Blue and White were adopted as the school colors; and, although there were other crises to overcome along the way, Dakota University—renamed Dakota Wesleyan in 1904 to avoid confusion with the state university in Vermillion—survived and thrived into its second century.

Meanwhile, there were other developments in Mitchell and throughout the county. In 1883 the first courthouse was completed, but not without controversy. County citizens—still relatively few in number—had approved the expenditure of $20,000 for the structure by a vote of 264 to 56. A contract was awarded to Henry H. Calhoun as both architect and builder, but when he failed to perform, the commissioners paid him off and supervised the job themselves.

Of greater excitement, however, was the formation of the Southeastern Dakota Agricultural and Driving Park Association, a group of horse racing enthusiasts who built a track and stables east of Mitchell. Harness racing was in vogue at the time, and trotters from throughout the Midwest participated in the meets which first began in 1882. They were gala affairs which brought diversion from the

The Southeastern Dakota Agricultural and Driving Park Association established a race track and stables east of Mitchell in 1882. The site later became a city park named for Abner E. Hitchcock. Mitchell Area Historical Society.

seriousness of establishing schools, businesses, churches and homesteads. (It's getting ahead of the story, but the Driving Park later became the site for several territorial fairs; the track was used for auto racing; and eventually the land was converted into a city park named for pioneer lawyer Abner E. Hitchcock, one of the original purchasers who later served as mayor.)

While all this was going on, the railroad was a key factor in the area's development. Immigrant cars brought in homesteaders with their livestock and meager possessions. Boxcars hauled out surplus grain which boosted the local economy. In September of 1884 several hundred people gathered in Mitchell for the laying of the cornerstone of the Milwaukee Road's new brick roundhouse with its stalls for fourteen engines. It was a social event as well as a symbolic indication of the town's recognition as a growing transportation hub. Literally scores of families depended on the railroad for their livelihood, and the Milwaukee Road's payroll went a long way towards supporting local businesses.

The roundhouse whistle had an important though somewhat ominous role. It was the signal for the Mitchell Hook and Ladder Company No. 1 to spring into action with carts, buckets and hoses to fight a fire somewhere in town. Formation of the company preceded the roundhouse by two years, and volunteers practiced regularly,

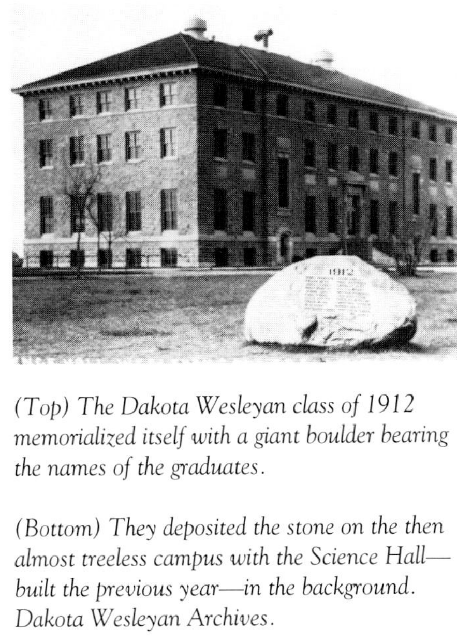

(Top) The Dakota Wesleyan class of 1912 memorialized itself with a giant boulder bearing the names of the graduates.

(Bottom) They deposited the stone on the then almost treeless campus with the Science Hall—built the previous year—in the background. Dakota Wesleyan Archives.

(Top) *Before Whittier School was built in 1880 at a cost of $7,000, Mitchell students attended classes in the Presbyterian chapel. Whittier, which served both elementary and high school students, was moved when Central School was erected on the same site in 1895. Mitchell Area Historical Society.*

(Bottom) *The J. F. Anderson Lumber Company of Mitchell was a major supplier of building materials for the area. The giant steam tractor in the foreground was prepared to deliver a five-wagon "train" of heavy timbers to a construction site. Mitchell Area Historical Society.*

pulling carts, coupling hoses and scaling ladders. Supposedly, if a member missed practice, he was fined 25 cents. In time the company acquired two white mares which were so well trained that they responded to the whistle as quickly as the men, positioning themselves alongside the tongue of the fire wagon so they could be harnessed in seconds.

Even before the roundhouse was completed, though, the company was called out for the town's first major fire. The First National Bank at Second and Main was in flames, and although the firefighters managed to control the spread of the blaze, the bank was a total loss.

Throughout the 1880s the young towns of Davison County acquired the basic needs of thriving communities. Newspapers, stores, schools, churches, social and fraternal clubs, banks and, yes, saloons were established. To counter the latter, ladies joined the Women's Christian Temperance Union and vehemently decried the evils of alcohol. Mitchell's first library was in a shack at First and South Main, its books contributed by the Presbyterian minister, Reverend M. E. Chapin, and consisting mostly of philosophical works which hardly anybody wanted to read. Reverend Chapin also deeded a building to house the Young Men's Christian Association which was incorporated in 1885 with 65 cents in its treasury. Elsewhere, Ethan was still in its infancy, and Mount Vernon was recovering from its disastrous fire, but despite the drouth and hard times which prevailed across South Dakota, there was an underlying optimism among the hardy folks who struggled throughout the economic doldrums and capricious weather into a new decade.

A cruise down the Jim River to Rockport aboard Jim Tobin's Capital *was a summer-time treat in the early 1900s. Upstream travel was curtailed by the dam at White's Mill. Mitchell Area Historical Society.*

When the Mount Vernon School was opened in 1883, the lower story was used for classes and the upper as a lodge room, opera house and temporary church. It burned in 1917. Mitchell Area Historical Society.

(Top) In 1902 county teachers attended an "Institute" at the new Mitchell High School, so designated by the Latin inscription "Schola Alta" above the entry. Young girls supposedly wrote the number 18 on the bottom of their shoes so that when they were interviewed for a teaching job, they could honestly say they were "over 18," the minimum age. Florence Althen collection.

(Bottom) After the destructive fire of 1889, Mount Vernon rebuilt and continued to add new business houses on Main Street, expecting major growth which never came. Mount Vernon Library.

Mitchellites turned out in force for the laying of the cornerstone of the Milwaukee Road's brick roundhouse with stalls for fourteen locomotives. Mitchell was known by railroaders as an "orange and black" town because of the dominant presence of the C.M.&St.P. Mitchell Area Historical Society.

The Chicago, Milwaukee & St. Paul Railway Company's depot on the south end of Mitchell's Main Street was a continuing hub of activity during the era when there were two or more passenger trains daily. Horse-drawn hacks met every arrival, day or night. Mitchell Area Historical Society/Ole Leeland photo.

In 1897 John and Carl Althen's threshing rig with steam tractor was typical of the equipment then used in the grain fields of Davison County. Elevators at all the railroad towns, including Betts and Loomis, provided shipping outlets for crops of wheat, oats, barley and flax. Florence Althen collection.

Horse-drawn hacks were the taxicabs of the era when every town of any size had one or more livery stables like the one on Second Avenue in Mitchell. Holy Family Catholic Church, completed in 1906, is shown in the background. Mitchell Area Historical Society.

In 1881 Mitchell's police force consisted of Marshal Frank Stiles whose duties were primarily that of a night watchman. Additional officers, in the uniforms of their era, kept pace with the growth of the city. J. Leonard Jennewein photo collection with the N. J. Dunham manuscript, Layne Library, Dakota Wesleyan University.

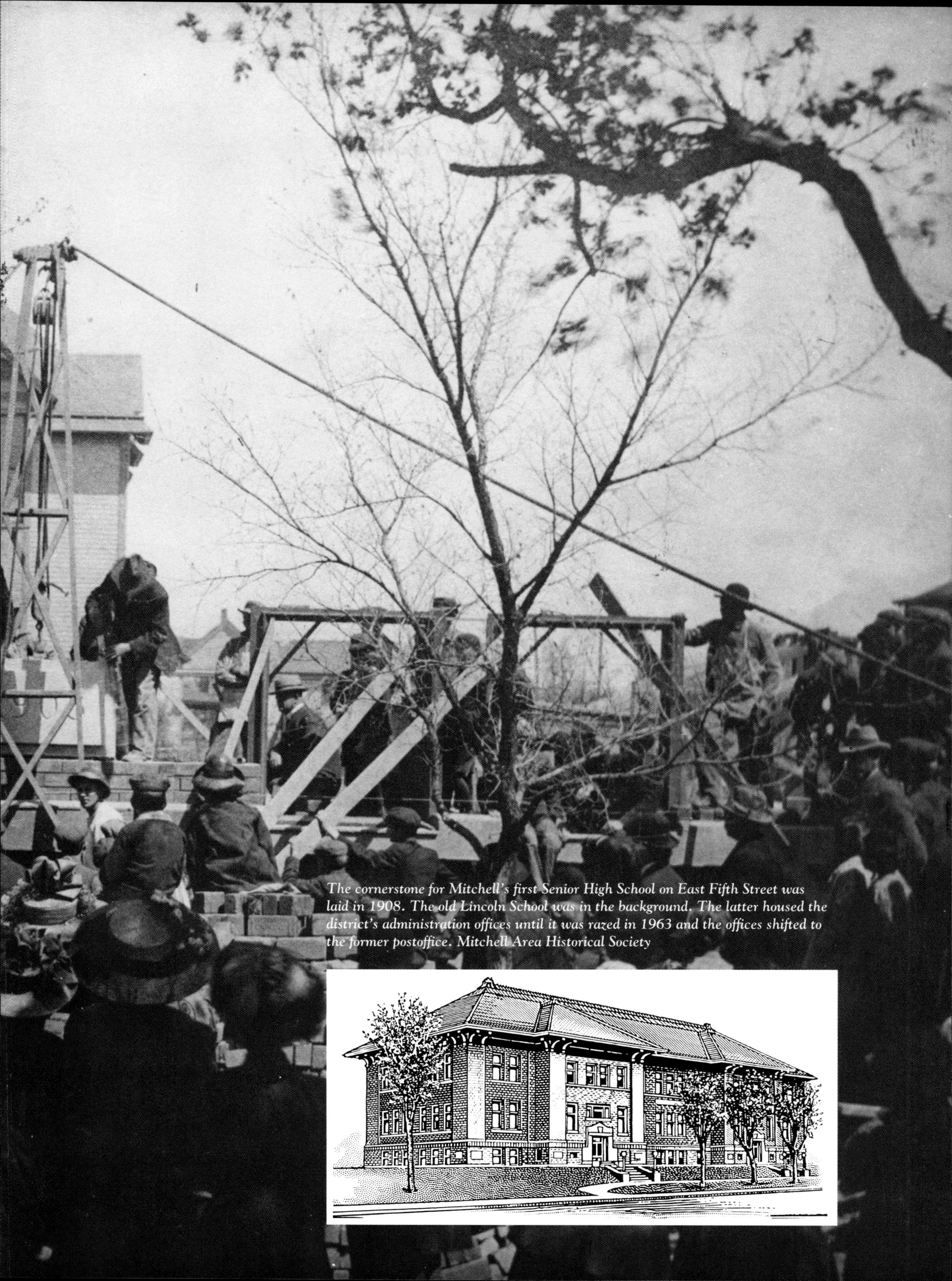

The cornerstone for Mitchell's first Senior High School on East Fifth Street was laid in 1908. The old Lincoln School was in the background. The latter housed the district's administration offices until it was razed in 1963 and the offices shifted to the former postoffice. Mitchell Area Historical Society

L. D GALE
DRUGGIST,
JEWELER,
AND
Bookseller.

CHAPTER 5

A Palace of Corn and a Capital Fight

Mitchell suffered no lack of civic promoters in its early years. In 1882 the previously mentioned Board of Trade (which later evolved into the Chamber of Commerce) was organized with a membership including some of the same names of the Driving Park Association founders. Presumably the board offered a liberal bonus to a Monmouth, Illinois, company to erect a rolling mill and elevator with a daily capacity of 125 barrels of flour. With similar encouragement, the Toledo (Ohio) Linseed Oil Company built a warehouse to buy flax from area farmers with a goal of producing a hundred barrels of oil a day. The Board of Trade also was involved in the construction of a large foundry and machine shop to manufacture iron pumps and other industrial equipment. An oatmeal plant and a rope factory were high on its priority list.

It was this kind of collective drive and imagination which eventually led to Mitchell's major attraction. Through the years there have been conflicting claims about who first conceived the idea of a corn palace as a showcase for the county's agricultural bounty. Lore has it that Lawrence O. Gale, the pioneer druggist, and Louis E. Beckwith were key figures in the venture, but there were others involved, too. A multi-county organization called the Corn Belt Real Estate Association was intent on promoting further settlement in the region and envisioned a fall harvest festival to emphasize the productivity of the land.

The corn palace idea was not new. The small town of Plankinton on the railroad line west of Mitchell had boasted a somewhat limited grain-decorated hall in 1890. Three years earlier Sioux City, Iowa, had unveiled an elaborately festooned structure with towers and turrets to which the regal name was applied. Thousands of visitors came to see it during its brief existence, including President Grover Cleveland. The Sioux City palace actually was a temporary building which was taken down after the celebration each year. In 1891 the expense of the Mexican National Band created financial trouble for the promoters. Consequently, in the following year—faced with the costs of erection, plus other difficulties, including a flood—the Sioux Citians decided to abandon their popular attraction.

That, of course, left an obvious void, and the Mitchell boosters took advantage of the opportunity. Gale and Beckwith visited the

(Opposite page) Lawrence O. Gale, the driving force behind the original Corn Palace, was a master promoter. The costume of this model was covered with jewelry items sold in his store. Mitchell Area Historical Society.

(Top) This panoramic view looking east on 3rd Avenue and the camera's north-south distortion of Main Street featured the Alexander Mitchell Hotel with its distinctive mansard roof on one corner and the Commercial and Savings Bank on the other. The turrets of the 1907 Corn Palace can be seen in the distance at the left. Mitchell Area Historical Society.

(Bottom) William Jennings Bryan (in rear seat of carriage in the foreground) was one of three presidential candidates to speak in Mitchell on consecutive days in 1908. The "Great Commoner" addressed a huge crowd for two hours, but he lost the election to William Howard Taft, who was so hoarse when he appeared that he could hardly be heard. Mitchell Area Historical Society.

Iowa river town to learn as much as they could about the building and the festival. Their report was greeted with enthusiasm by the Corn Belt Realtors Association, and the decision was made to move full speed ahead.

Andrew J. Kings was contracted to erect a 66-by-100 foot arena on the southeast corner of Fourth and Main at an eventual cost of $2,976.48. John Lawler, with his railroad connections, arranged for numerous special trains with reduced fares to bring in visitors and potential land-buyers. Colonel Alexander Rohe, a Kansas designer who had decorated the Sioux City palace, was hired to add the artistic touches to the hall's exterior with colored corn, native grasses and other grains, while local ladies embellished the interior. A total of $3,700 was raised to get the project off to a solvent beginning. In the meantime, Lawrence Gale had arranged for Professor Paul P. Phinney's Iowa State Boys' Band as the featured musical attraction, and sixteen counties agreed to provide agricultural exhibits.

On September 28, 1892—just two months after the wheels started turning—the first Corn Belt Exposition was opened to a receptive public. So successful was the ten-day celebration that an encore was planned for 1893 in the building enlarged by a 42-foot addition. This time a nationally known military band from Lynn, Massachusetts, was hired, and another large crowd attended the extravaganza. Mitchell, it seemed, had found an entertainment gemstone to set her apart from other South Dakota towns—but then unforeseen circumstances intervened.

The Panic of 1893—blamed by President Cleveland on excessive cheap paper money—struck South Dakota somewhat belatedly and came in combination with a searing drouth the following summer which matched or exceeded any of the previous dry spells since the earliest territorial days. Davison County suffered along with the rest of the state, and in Mitchell the committee in charge decided to cancel the 1894 Corn Belt Exposition.

The hiatus lasted for six years, even though the rains came, economic conditions improved and the Spanish-American War generated patriotic fervor. In 1900 the festival was revived, however, with Lawrence Gale again heading the sponsoring organization. Presidential candidate William Jennings Bryan, the foremost orator of the day, drew visitors from all over the state, the *Mitchell Republican* estimating the crowd at 10,000, while the *Sioux Falls Press* doubled that figure for the 35-minute speech. Mitchell was not quite ready to accept the Corn Belt Exposition as a permanent event, though, and the 1901 show was not held.

Another bit of Mitchell lore is that the genesis of the Corn Palace as a continuing annual spectacle supposedly took place at a surprise birthday party for Thomas Fullerton, the pioneer lumberyard operator and former mayor. The guests talked about the city's future—possibly as the state's capital—and they agreed that the off-and-on-again exposition should be revived. The next morning some of them visited Lawrence Gale and persuaded him to take on the chairmanship again. After some hesitation, he did, and the 1902 show was assured.

Gale traveled to Chicago to book DeBaugh's 20th Century Band. Meanwhile, another key figure in the story—Dr. Robert F. Dundas, a physician who just happened to have his office in Gale's drugstore—assumed the responsibility for getting the building refurbished. That year members of the committee went to Pierre to file articles of incorporation for the Corn Belt Exposition, and from then on the autumn festival became a continuing event. In 1905 the Corn Palace name replaced the Corn Belt designation.

The original Corn Palace was photographed by Jerome Wiltse who was given exclusive rights by the committee. Lawrence E. Stair, a competitor, objected and took pictures of the building—as the story goes—from behind a fence. Wiltse's exclusive permission was soon withdrawn, and in the ensuing century, literally millions of photos have been taken of the three different Palaces. Mitchell Area Historical Society/ Jerome Wiltse photo.

While a year-by-year account of the celebration is precluded in this volume, at least three special episodes deserve mention. The first came in 1904 when Mitchellites helped persuade the legislature to put the nagging question of the state capital location to the vote of the people for the third time since 1889. Mitchell became Pierre's chief contender on the theory that being nearer the center of population was more important than being at the geographic midpoint. The referendum was a serious blow to the Hughes County town which was still heavily in debt from an earlier election. However, it was time to settle the issue once and for all, so the campaign got underway in earnest.

The Milwaukee Road (serving Mitchell) and the Chicago & North Western (serving Pierre) got into the fight, providing free transportation for all South Dakotans wishing to visit the competing towns. An estimated 100,000 passes were issued before the election was over. Hotel and restaurant accommodations were unable to keep up with the trainloads of curious guests, and so local residents were called upon to share their homes and their larders with potential voters.

As an additional lure, the Mitchell city council offered the new three-story city hall—built of red quartzite at a cost of $55,000—as a temporary capitol. (It later served its original purpose until it was

In 1901 the Mitchell Fire Department won state championship honors. Firefighters throughout the county's history had many opportunities to put their training into practice. Mitchell Area Historical Society.

The Corn Palace's distinctive towers and Moorish minarets were finally added in 1937 under the direction of Floyd Kings, son of the builder of the first structure 45 years earlier. The onion-shaped domes restored the uniqueness of appearance which characterized the first two Palaces. Mitchell Area Historical Society.

(Left) William Howard Taft's appearance in Mitchell in 1908 was marred by his loss of voice, but he was well received and eventually defeated William Jennings Bryan and Eugene Chapin for the presidency. Mitchell Area Historical Society.

(Bottom) In 1904 during the competition with Pierre for the seat of state government, Mitchell offered its new three-story city hall as a tem-porary capitol as one of its inducements. After the election was lost, the red quartzite structure served its original purpose until it was razed in 1960. Clyde Goin collection.

Farmer's Day on February 21, 1935, was typical of the multiple use of the Corn Palace. It was part of a Good Roads Fair during the heart of the Dirty Thirties. Mitchell Area Historical Society/Harry B. Hershey photo.

razed in 1960.) For two months the expensive and wearying effort continued as a carnival atmosphere prevailed in both towns which tried to out-entertain each other. The Corn Palace was a plus factor which Pierre could not duplicate, and the committee decided to take full advantage of it by going after John Philip Sousa and his world famous band. Chairman Gale sent a wire to Frank Christianer, Sousa's manager, inquiring what it would cost to bring the composer and his musicians to South Dakota. Christianer apparently thought he was dealing with rubes from the hinterlands and expected his reply to scare them off. However, Gale sent another telegram asking for specific charges for two concerts daily for six days; and when the proffered terms were declared acceptable, Christianer came to Mitchell to double-check the request. When he learned that local banks were backing the contract, he signed the papers and supposedly said: "Whatever you gentlemen lack in judgment, you certainly make up in nerve."

When the noted bandmaster arrived at the Mitchell station and saw the size of the town and the unpaved streets, the story goes that he refused to leave the train until he got paid in advance. Bankers then counted out the cash and delivered it in sacks to the astounded conductor. Not only did Sousa fulfill his commitment, but he added extra performances and encores. (When he was invited back three years later, he accepted readily with apparent delight.)

The committee, in the meantime, had denied Pierre representatives the right to set up their exhibit in the Corn Palace, so they had to be satisfied with space in a downtown hotel. In the end, though, Mitchell's aggressive effort was all for naught. Sousa was a great success, but with heavy Black Hills support and the backing of other South Dakotans who were tired of the repeated resurrection of the removal question, Pierre retained the seat of government by a vote of 58,617 to 41,155.

In 1905 the Business Men's League of Mitchell, which had succeeded the Corn Belt Realtors Association as principal backers of the annual exposition, decided that the original building should be torn down and replaced with a larger hall to accommodate the ever-increasing crowds. Doctor Dundas was put in charge of the construction at the new site on the northeast corner of Main Street and Fifth Avenue. The 125-by-142 foot structure was completed in 55 days at a cost of $15,000, in time for the appearance of the Italian Banda Rosa (Red Band). Despite a profitable show, the committee ended the year with a $7,500 debt.

In 1906—after he had booked the Kilties bagpipe band from Scotland for the Corn Palace—the irrepressible Lawrence Gale built the Gale Theater, reputedly the finest in the state. As it turned out, it was one of the reasons why the 1907 exposition lost money, even though John Philip Sousa was back for a return engagement. Gale, who moved to Minneapolis with his family that year, had turned his theatre over to Maurice W. Jencks who staged a competing program which affected attendance at the Palace. At the same time, three days of horse races at the Driving Park caused further reduction in gate receipts. A $600 loss was added to the previous indebtedness and caused some nervousness among the committee members.

Contractor Andrew J. Kings, builder of the First Corn Palace, had his office in the right one-third of the one-story brick building next to C. I. Anderson's planing mill at First and Kimball in Mitchell. In 1919 the same limited space was the original home of Tessier's, Inc., which grew into a major heating and air-conditioning firm. Evan Tessier collection.

BALDWIN GRAND

With William M. Smith succeeding Gale as chairman, the committee vowed to make its 1908 King Korn festival "the grandest carnival week in the west." Thavius' Band from Chicago was the featured musical organization for the Palace program, and the free outdoor acts included the Araki Japanese acrobatic troupe and McGarver's colored singers and dancers. Street bands came from Avon, Stickney, Bridgewater and Redfield. The big attraction, though, was the presence of the three leading candidates for the presidency of the United States appearing on consecutive days.

First to arrive was the Great Commoner, William Jennings Bryan, the Democratic nominee whose booming voice had been heard in Mitchell before. This time he spoke for two hours to a huge crowd estimated by the Democratic *Gazette* at more than 20,000. On the second day the Republican candidate, William Howard Taft, then the Secretary of War, arrived, suffering from a severe throat problem which the *Sanborn County Herald* reported thusly:

Judge Taft was as hoarse as a frog when he spoke in Woonsocket . . . but people say it was worth driving 40 miles just to see him smile and hear him croak. That's the difference between Mr. Taft and Bryan. Bryan hollers himself black in the face and people don't believe a word he says. Bill Taft doesn't say much . . . but people know he means what he says.

In Mitchell Taft spoke for about three-quarters of an hour, but

(Opposite page) The Palace was—and continues to be—utilized for a wide variety of promotions, concerts, conventions and other events. (below) The original Corn Palace was wired for exterior lights for the first time in 1909. Twenty years later Harry B. Hersey took this night-time shot of the third building before domes and turrets were added. Mitchell Area Historical Society.

The championship game of the 1923 state high school basketball tournament was held in the Corn Palace before a full-house crowd of 5,000 as the Yankton Bucks defeated the Mitchell Kernels 25-14. The defensive alignment at the tipoff, although somewhat lost in the glare off the floor, was considerably different from that of later-day tactics. Through the years the Palace played host to hundreds of sports events. Mitchell Area Historical Society/Harry B. Hersey photo.

the papers said only three or four thousand people in the crowd of "between 25,000 and 30,000" as reported by the *Sioux Falls Argus-Leader* were able to hear him because of his hoarseness—but they cheered anyhow. Later at Yankton he said he had lost part of his voice at the Corn Palace and portions of it were scattered all along the line from Mitchell. By the time he reached Elk Point, he was unable to talk above a whisper.

The third candidate was Eugene Wilder Chapin representing the Prohibition Party who addressed a gathering of some 2,000-3,000 people in front of the Corn Palace, his audience including a good representation of the Women's Christian Temperance Union active in the city and surrounding towns. He drew chuckles and cheers when he said:

"The three candidates may be classed as follows: Mr. Bryan is the Peerless Leader, Mr. Taft is the Fearless Leader and I am the Beerless Leader."

When the votes were in, "Bill" Taft carried the state and succeeded Teddy Roosevelt as the 27th President. The appearance of the three candidates proved a financial boon for the Corn Palace. There was no further question about its permanency, and two years later its debt was paid off and the committee ritualistically burned the loan papers.

The third episode of note occurred a dozen years later. Once again the Corn Palace was proving too small to accommodate its audiences. Besides that, state fire laws helped force the issue, and in 1919 a decision was made to build a new brick arena with year-round use possibilities to replace the unheated wooden structure. The original Palace had been at Fourth and Main, the second—completed in 1905—at Fifth and Main, and the latest—planned for the 1920 exposition—would be at Sixth and Main as the Palace moved north-

Boys' bands were special favorites of Corn Palace audiences in the earlier years as they gave free outdoor concerts and marched in midway parades. Girls were excluded because as late as the 1920s it was still considered unladylike for them to play instruments other than violins, pianos, cellos, organs or harps. Mitchell Area Historical Society.

(Above) Famed Sioux artist Oscar Howe (left) designed the Corn Palace decorations for many years, including in his unusual artistry this image of Lawrence Welk which he pointed out to the popular Champagne Music maestro. Welk and his entertainers played the Palace five times, more than any other organization. Mitchell Area Historical Society/Dorothy Prather

(Top, right) Helen Gross was selected as queen of the 1915 Corn Palace exposition and crowned by Mayor Abner Hitchcock with fitting ceremony. Choosing the queen by having candidates compete in a corn-picking contest was a short-lived idea. Mitchell Area Historical Society

ward block by block. Mitchell voters approved a $100,000 bond issue to cover half the costs by a vote of 1,129 to 231.

Unfortunately, there were delays in planning and construction so that it was necessary to hold the 1920 exposition in a large circus tent. There were no decorations and the weather turned cold, making it uncomfortable for both performers and audience. However, a feeling of expectation for the following year prevailed, and the new building—adorned with a post-war theme of disarmament—did not disappoint Palace enthusiasts. Governor William H. McMasters gave the dedication speech, and Karl L. King, with his 60-piece band, introduced the "Corn Palace March" which he composed for the occasion.

The saga of one of the nation's most unique buildings is worthy of book-length telling by itself, but in the broader context of Davison County's overall history, only an abbreviated account is possible.

Through the years hundreds of volunteers have been involved, and the sometimes laughable, sometimes worrisome and occasionally best forgotten incidents have been virtually endless. Its entertainment bills have included a lengthy litany of famous performers, among them Paul Whiteman, Tommy and Jimmy Dorsey, Lawrence Welk, Harry James, Guy Lombardo, Duke Ellington, Tennessee Ernie Ford, the King Sisters, Andy Williams, Patti Page, Eddy Arnold, Andy Griffith, Jack Benny, Red Skelton, Bob Hope and even the Three Stooges.

Besides the headliners there were other performers on the Main Street midway as well as visiting celebrities on the Palace stage. In 1925 Gutzon Borglum came to explain his plan for Mount Rushmore. A year later Secretary of Commerce Herbert Hoover gave two addresses, and in 1932 Congresswoman Ruth Bryan Owens, daughter of William Jennings Bryan, spoke to commemorate her father's earlier appearances. In 1935 the Hilton Siamese twins shared the entertainment bill with the Herbie Kay Orchestra, and 160 sets of twins from South Dakota responded to an invitation to attend a special performance with the two co-joined sisters.

In 1908 Dr. Floyd Gillis, son of the Ethan pioneer and former assistant to Colonel Rohe, the original designer, took over the decorating responsibilities for the Palace. A graduate of Dakota Wesleyan and with a medical degree from the University of Michigan, Gillis

(Below, left) Erecting the scaffolding to decorate the second Corn Palace building was almost as intricate a job as the design work itself. Because of all the grain used in the process, the Palace was often referred to as the "world's largest bird feeder." Mitchell Area Historical Society.

(Bottom, left) Red Skelton was one of the most popular of Corn Palace entertainers. He came early for his scheduled appearance and circulated among the Midway crowd, delighting visitors, signing autographs and generally enjoying himself. Mitchell Area Historical Society.

(Below) Many visitors had their pictures taken in the fake balloon flight "over" the Corn Palace. It was a popular souvenir in 1911. Eight decades later Mitchell would be the site of a world-class balloon and airship museum. Jean Geyerman collection.

Each year thousands of South Dakotans and out-of-state visitors have flocked to Mitchell for the annual Corn Palace festival, not only to attend the stage shows featuring big-name entertainers but to enjoy the carnival atmosphere on Main Street. Mitchell Area Historical Society.

The Corn Palace was a plus factor for Mitchell in the 1904 competition for the state capital. Pierre was denied use of the building for its promotional display, but despite all the efforts by the Davison County promoters, Mitchell lost the election by 7,462 votes out of 99,772 ballots cast. J. Leonard Jennewein photo collection with the N. J. Dunham manuscript, Layne Library, Dakota Wesleyan University.

The first two Corn Palaces were made of wood and unheated. The third (opposite page) was designed for year-around use and has hosted hundreds of varied events besides the annual festival. Included were St. Joseph's Hospital's charity ball in 1923 (above). Queen of Peace Hospital collections/Harry B. Hersey photos.

held the job until 1917 when he went into military service in World War I. During his tenure his greatest crisis apparently came in 1912 when his workers went on strike and high school boys had to be hired to finish the task in time for the festival.

Architect Floyd Kings followed Gillis and was succeeded, in turn, by William Kearney who stayed at it for three decades, through the added difficulties of war-time and the Dirty Thirties. His successor—from 1948 to 1971—was the Yanktonai Sioux artist, Oscar Howe, after which the tradition was carried on by local art teachers Barbara Young, Don Durfee and Cal Schultz. An elaborate design around the stage proscenium was created by another Indian artist, Arthur Amiotte.

Each year some 300 or more bushels of colored corn and two tons of grain have embellished the building while also providing a bountiful banquet for mice, squirrels, sparrows and pigeons before reasonably adequate controls were devised. One year the pigeons got so bad that workmen reportedly captured 800 of them in a single night. Needless to say, the Palace is occasionally referred to as "the world's largest bird feeder."

Of more serious concern, though, were the senseless attempts by one or more arsonists in the 1970s to destroy the building. The worst of three blazes on June 21, 1979, caused extensive damage to the roof and front exterior. Remnants of one of the fiberglass domes weighing almost a ton fell to the ground and had to be replaced. (Earlier domes

State fire laws and a desire for a permanent year-around arena resulted in the third Corn Palace completed too late for the 1920 exposition which had to be held in a tent. Except for the artistic grain panels, the building tended to look more like an auditorium than a regal edifice. Mitchell Area Historical Society.

Paving Sixth Avenue alongside the third Corn Palace in the 1920s required men and muscle. The crushed rock base was laid with wheelbarrows, while bags of cement and sand were hand-loaded into the crude mixer. Materials were hauled to the site from the railroad yard by team and wagon. Mitchell Area Historical Society.

or minarets were of concrete and were so heavy that they threatened structural damage to the roof.)

Through it all, however, the Corn Palace survived. In 1976 when ticket prices were raised to a top of ten dollars, the Bob Hope show produced the greatest profit for a single year. After that, though, skyrocketing costs began to have negative effects on the ledger, beginning with the Rich Little/Victor Borge split engagement in 1978 and continuing with the Mills Brothers/Jim Nabors in 1979,

Among its early-day industries, Mitchell had a rug factory operated by Dedrick and Susan LaMotte, the latter shown at the loom. Note the Christmas bells giving a limited festive appearance to the cramped work place. Mitchell Area Historical Society.

To decorate the Corn Palace anew each year, ears of varied colored corn are cut in half lengthwise and nailed to coded design patterns, not unlike painting by the numbers. Mitchell Area Historical Society.

(Above) The 1924 Mitchell Automobile Show featured an airplane on the Corn Palce stage. (below) A 4-H rally drew young club members from throughout the state. Mitchell Area Historical Society.

Bill Anderson/Brenda Lee in 1980, Burl Ives/Ernie Ford in 1981 and Red Skelton in 1982. The entertainment business, like so many other things, had undergone a big change with rock-and-roll music, Baby Boomers and the increased competition of television.

Trying to predict public tastes thus became a dilemma for the later-day Corn Palace committee members which L. O. Gale and the festival pioneers did not have to face.

UTOCYCLE'S
RIDE A
HARLEY-DAVI
MOTO
SOLD BY GEORGE H. SPRY.
THE FLYING

CHAPTER 6

A Bit of Scandal—and a New Century

By comparison with some of the other counties in the state, Davison in its early years was relatively free of major crimes, murders and scandals. In its edition of March 19, 1879, the *Yankton Press and Dakotaian* reported: "Horsethiefs [*sic*] are operating in the vicinity of Firesteel . . . where they have to put their horses under lock and key at night." There was no later mention of catching or "stringing up" the culprits.

On April 9, 1884, the bad-tempered keeper of the Parlour Saloon, Henry N. Lewis, shot and killed the Mitchell city marshal, John T. Pierce, when the latter tried to quell a disturbance in the bar three hours after the legal closing time. Lewis fled but was arrested by Deputy Sheriff Dan Collins and charged with murder. Some say he married the woman who was the chief witness, and as his wife, she was not compelled to testify against him. His attorney got his trial shifted to Plankinton where he pleaded self-defense, and with no testimony against him, he was acquitted.

Without doubt, the most sensational affair to erupt in the county had its beginnings in 1886 and involved John D. Lawler and Robert H. McBride, publisher of the *Mitchell Mail*. The two men had been friends and active fellow Democrats, although Lawler knew that McBride was twice divorced and had a reputation for unsavory journalistic tactics. The problem occurred when the newspaperman announced that he was going to marry Nina S. Dousman, Lawler's well-to-do widowed sister-in-law. Concerned for her future, the Mitchell banker informed Nina of McBride's past, and the latter heard about it.

Nina did not accept her brother-in-law's advice and married the publisher anyway. McBride turned the *Mail* over to his brother John and lived out of the state on his wife's largesse until she discovered that he was frequenting high-class houses of prostitution and apparently tried to steal some of her jewelry. She hired a detective to have him followed, and in 1891—despite her Catholic religion and the fact that they had a young daughter—she won an uncontested divorce. McBride then returned to Mitchell and resumed management of the *Mail*.

That's when he began an editorial vendetta against the First National Bank president. In issue after issue he carried on his vitri-

(Opposite page and following page) Motorcycles joined horseless carriages on the streets of Mitchell before World War I. Capitalizing on the booming market was George H. Spry who sold Harley-Davidsons, Excelsiors and Flying Merkels. Mitchell Area Historical Society.

Friends of John Lawler demolished the office of Robert McBride's Mitchell Mail *in retaliation for the newspaper-man's vindictive crusade against the banker. The bitter feud and ensuing court action dragged on for years, even after Lawler's death. J. Leonard Jennewein photo collection with the N. J. Dunham manuscript, Layne Library, Dakota Wesleyan University.*

olic attack, with sneering remarks about Lawler and his family and, in every way possible, hinting that the banker was dishonest and that his institution was on the verge of failure. Lawler became so incensed at one time that he assaulted McBride in the latter's office, although no particular damage to either party was reported. Then, to add fuel to the fire, the publisher filed a $50,000 alienation of affection suit against his ex-brother-in-law. The case was dismissed, and McBride had to pay Lawler's court costs of $70.35.

He then continued his vicious onslaught in the *Mail* and was quoted in another paper as saying: "If I have to live on one meal a week, I shall not let up on John D. Lawler till I drive him to a pauper's grave." Although not a pauper, on February 18, 1896, Lawler died in his sleep at a Sioux City, Iowa, hotel while on a business trip. His death—at age 42—was attributed to a heart attack, but many Mitchellites believed that stress over McBride's incessant slander had taken its toll.

The story did not end there, however. While other editors in Mitchell and across the state lauded Lawler, McBride took a final swipe at him in his obituary, even insinuating that the bank was in so much trouble that its president had turned to drink. This parting blow was too much for Lawler's friends, and on February 24 more than four dozen of them (including Abner Hitchcock, the park donor) invaded the *Mail* office above Dr. Rodell C. Warne's drugstore. While McBride was hiding in the physician's locked office, they hauled his printing equipment into the street and burned it while someone took a sledge hammer to his press.

They got their revenge, but still the scandalous episode continued. There were repercussions for and against the attackers. The bank was closed for 30 days while an examiner checked out McBride's allegations which proved unfounded. William H. Knowles, a pioneer grocer who had participated in the raid, committed suicide, and there was divided opinion as to whether it was because of remorse or some other reason. Then the ex-publisher sued all the vengeance-seekers for a considerable sum. After an extended trial, a jury agreed that his property had been destroyed but awarded him only $700, although the 35 defendants were assessed court costs and legal fees.

In what some termed poetic justice, exactly two months after the trial ended—on February 1, 1901—McBride, like his foe, collapsed

The Mount Vernon Fire Department hose-laying team competed in the state competition in Rapid City. Victim of several costly blazes, the town desperately needed trained and dedicated volunteers to prevent further losses. Mount Vernon Library.

(Top) In 1907 Fred M. and Will Johnson, cabinet and violin makers from Sweden, started their own furniture store. They survived the Dirty Thirties by selling washing machines for a dollar down and a dollar a week, and eventually became one of the oldest family-owned businesses in Mitchell. Johnson Furniture Company.

(Bottom) The Mitchell branch of Hess Rau and Company, a plumbing firm, displayed bathtubs and other fixtures in its combination office and showroom in 1909. John H. Giese was the resident manager and later owner. Mitchell Area Historical Society.

The Mt. Vernon Merchandise Company was established in 1894 by Mark C. Betts who operated it until 1923. He also was co-founder of the Mount Vernon News *and served two terms in the state legislature. Wally Scott collection.*

and died of a heart attack at age 58. According to historian Robert H. Lee, who wrote an extensive review of the case in the *South Dakota History* magazine, it took until 1906 for all of the defendants to pay up their share of the judgment. In the end, it cost each of them $26.38 to rid Mitchell of the *Mail* and McBride.

Meanwhile, during the fifteen years this protracted soap opera was being played out, Davison County grew and prospered. The census of 1900 showed a population of 7,483, of whom 4,055 were in Mitchell, but the small towns were active, too. As a grain-shipping point, Mount Vernon with its four elevators eclipsed the county seat. "Prairie Lily" and "Takota" flour produced by the Mount Vernon Milling Company found markets throughout the state.

In 1896 the Mount Vernon Cooperative Creamery was established with Herman H. Garey in charge, creating an industry which would later be duplicated in Ethan and Mitchell. The creameries provided a source of ready cash for county farmers and helped many of them through difficult times. The Mount Vernon Telephone Company was organized by Depot Agent C. B. Woodward, who was also instrumental in bringing electric lights to the town in 1912. He later added an artificial ice plant. A water works had been completed in November of 1904, but it was not in time for Mount Vernon's second big fire. The elevators and a warehouse were destroyed, and only the arrival of the Mitchell Fire Department on a special train saved the

The horseless carriage craze hit Davison County in the first decade of the 1900s as it did elsewhere throughout the country. New owners were eager to show off their steamers and gas buggies in parades and competitions. Automobile Day in Mitchell provided an opportunity for pioneer motorists to do just that. Mitchell Area Historical Society.

rest of the town. A year later Mount Vernon organized two firefighting companies of its own.

With the extension of the railroad northward from Mitchell, the town of Loomis was platted in 1902. There is some argument as to whether it was named for the builder of the first elevator, the Loomis Elevator Company of Minnesota or for L. N. Loomis, who was a state senator from Dell Rapids at the time. Whatever its true name derivation, Loomis gave evidence of becoming a boom town in 1908 when the William Galloway Company of Waterloo, Iowa, purchased 80 acres and began building a factory for the manufacture of automobiles and farm machinery with a promise of the eventual employment of 500 men. The Milwaukee Road planned for the enlarging of its depots and the building of side tracks—and then the bubble burst and Loomis never fulfilled the dream as its bank, hotel, general store, livery stable, four elevators and other vestiges of a thriving community folded and faded away.

A new age of dawning. Doctor Warne, who had used a bicycle to make professional calls in Mitchell, switched to a horseless carriage as did Dr. Byron A. Bobb who spent $800 in 1902 for a Locomobile steamer with no fenders, no windshield, no top and steered by a tiller. At the Driving Park a challenge race with horses was arranged, but the Locomobile failed to finish when its flues burned out. On another occasion the embarrassed doctor had to get a team to tow him home from Mount Vernon when his steamer broke down.

Because he and his fellow physicians had to spend so much time making house calls, Doctor Bobb appealed to the Presentation Sisters of Aberdeen to establish a hospital in Mitchell. They agreed, and with local support the nuns borrowed more than two-thirds of the $34,000 needed to complete a four-story wooden facility in 1906 in time to admit the first patient, Roy Metcalf, suffering from typhoid fever. By modern standards, conditions at St. Joseph's Hospital were crude indeed. Drinking water was brought from Cooney's Farm in barrels. Kerosene lamps and candles supplemented the undependable electric lights. A rope-operated elevator was used to reach the upper floors, and during the winter the building was so cold that the sisters and nurses packed the window sills with cotton to keep their patients reasonably warm. Payment for care was often made with chickens, eggs and vegetables—and for a time the hospital had its own flock of about 150 hens. Muddy streets and pathways led to the building because not until 1910 was a board sidewalk installed to connect it with Main Street.

Although Mitchell had an archaic telephone system briefly in the 1880s, local historians credit Fred B. Elce with establishing the town's first exchange in 1898. He hired his sister, Mrs. Walter Mayo, as the first operator. In 1904 he sold out to J. L. W. Zietlow's Dakota Central Telephone Company, after which there were extended battles over franchise rights which didn't end until the mid-1930s. About the same time the waterworks and sewage plant were upgraded, and the Mitchell Power Company provided improved electrical services to businesses and homes, making it possible for Doctor Dundas to have the Corn Palace wired and brightly lit with hundreds of bulbs in 1906.

The first decade of the twentieth century brought still other developments. In 1905 the Mitchell Bottling Works (which evolved into the Coca-Cola Bottling Company of Central South Dakota) had three employees who scrubbed bottles by hand in a wooden tub, filled them with pop, cider or near-beer and capped them with a pedal-operated machine at the rate of six bottles a minute. The Commercial Savings Bank (which became simply the Commercial Bank) ran into trouble in the construction of its new home at Third and Main when a partially completed, rain-softened wall collapsed. Masons working on the job escaped injury, but they had to start all over after the debris was hauled away. The impressive three-story building was completed in 1906, nine years after the bank's founding in 1897 by Howard R. Kibbee, Sr., George H. Rew, J. T. Morrow and Samuel Webber with a capital investment of $10,000.

Dr. Rodell C. Warne switched from a bicycle to a horseless carriage to make sick calls. He was a veteran of the Philippine insurrection campaign of 1899 and harbored Robert McBride when John Lawler's friends sacked the Mitchell Mail *office. Mitchell Area Historical Society.*

Throughout the county the so-called "Progressive Era" brought a period of prosperity and general well-being. Wooden buildings were replaced by structures of brick and stone. Automobiles became a common sight as livery stables gave way to garages and gas stations. Blacksmith Fred P. Grohs startled Ethan residents with his horseless carriage (a Rambler), and there were at least seven gasmobiles in Mount Vernon before the end of the first decade of the 1900s. In Mitchell, Dr. William A. Delaney, Sr., bought a Cartercar in 1912, the year the first streets in the town were paved. The fire department was then motorized with a Model T Ford hose truck. Daily passenger trains—often more than one—made the depots at Ethan, Mount Vernon, Mitchell and Loomis the exciting hubs of the communities. Old-timers met and talked of the pioneering days, but mostly the people looked ahead and not back.

659
C. M. & St P.

C. M. & St P.
65

(Above) On October 7, 1907, a Milwaukee Road freight train collided head-on with a switch engine pulling 21 cars on the main line in the Mitchell yard. Engineer Julius Plante and Floyd Bond, the switch engine fireman, jumped to safety from their locomotive after applying the brakes, but their counterparts in No. 659 were killed. J. Leonard Jennewein photo collection with the N. J. Dunham manuscript, Layne Library, Dakota Wesleyan University.

(Opposite page) Fortunately no one was killed or even injured when the Milwaukee Road bridge over the Jim River east of Mitchell collapsed. Despite the heavy traffic in and out of Davison County on the C.M.&St.P. and the Omaha lines, major accidents were relatively few. Mitchell Area Historical Society/Lawrence E. Stair photo.

(Top) With their numbers gradually dwindling, members of Mitchell's Grand Army of the Republic convened in 1912 to exchange stories of the Civil War of which they were veterans. J. Leonard Jennewein photo collection with the N. J. Dunham manuscript, Layne Library, Dakota Wesleyan University.

(Bottom) Loomis never fulfilled the dreams of its early residents and businessmen. This view of Main Street looking east towards the depot was indicative of the village's struggle for survival. Maxine Johnson collection.

(Top) Citizens of Loomis were proud of their school house with its bell tower; but, like the town itself, it faded into history, the victim of fire. Maxine Johnson collection.

(Bottom) Old settlers of the Ethan area posed for this 1911 photo in front of the then new Security State Bank, the same year the town's streets were graveled and cement sidewalks replaced many of the wooden ones. Note that clothing styles were as diverse as the individuals. J. Leonard Jennewein photo collection with the N. J. Dunham manuscript, Layne Library, Dakota Wesleyan University.

Partying Mitchellites rode to Mount Vernon for a Sunday dinner in this primitive motor-bus, said to be the first horseless carriage in the county. A four-piece band added to the jollity of the occasion. J. Leonard Jennewein photo collection with the N. J. Dunham manuscript, Layne Library, Dakota Wesleyan University.

The Lewis E. Scott garage, established in Mount Vernon in 1915, offered one-pump gas service during the transition period from horses to automobiles. Banker Herman H. Garey had the first car in town, a White Steamer. Wally Scott collection.

Duck hunting on the Jim River was highly productive when no limits were imposed. Davison County later attracted its share of nimrods pursuing the Chinese ringneck pheasant after the first official hunting season was inaugurated in 1919. Mitchell Area Historical Society.

Before the horseless carriage took over, bicycles offered a popular means of transportation for Davison County men and women. Pioneer photographer Lawrence E. Stair operated a bicycle sales and repair shop in Mitchell. J. Leonard Jennewein photo collection with the N. J. Dunham manuscript, Layne Library, Dakota Wesleyan University

Mount Vernon with its four elevators was the county's leading grain shipping point at the turn of the century. "Prairie Lily" and "Takota" flour produced by the town's milling company also provided a local market for farmers. J. Leonard Jennewein photo collection with the N. J. Dunham manuscript, Layne Library, Dakota Wesleyan University.

A general store was a fundamental institution for every viable small town. George Bauer's mercantile in Ethan also included a second-floor hall where dancing and roller skating parties were held. The building later was destroyed by fire. Note the display of corsets in the show window. Dorothy Feiner collection.

Banker Henry Zeier bought an open-air Buick from Ethan dealer William J. Smith as the automotive age reached Davison County. Livery stables were soon replaced by garages, and a demand for better roads followed. Leo and Sally Pollreisz collection.

Theodore F. King hauled cream from outlying stations to the Mount Vernon Creamery. In this turn-of-the-century photo, he was joined on the wagon by Reverend David Powell, a Methodist minister, who served in the last territorial and first state legislatures. Florence Althen collection.

There were sidewalk superintendents to spare when workmen began paving the street leading up to Mitchell's Milwaukee depot (top) and in front of the Widmann Hotel (bottom) prior to World War I. Mitchell Area Historical Society.

The Mitchell Elks Lodge at Fifth and Main was built in 1911 and was across the street from the second Corn Palace. It later became a church when the Elks moved elsewhere. Jean Geyerman collection.

Dray service in Mount Vernon was provided by Bill Constable with horse and wagon before the automotive age took over. The assessed valuation of the town in 1907 was $37,478, which included 83 horses at $3,140. Florence Althen collection.

John H. Giese (foreground), who established the Giese Plumbing Company in 1907, inspected the corner stakes for a new federal building which became the Mitchell postoffice and later a school administration building. The county courthouse is in the background. Mitchell Area Historical Society.

Most of the railroading emphasis in Davison County was on the Milwaukee Road, but the Chicago, St. Paul, Minneapolis and Omaha line connected Mitchell directly with Sioux Falls. The Chicago and North Western eventually took over what was always referred to as the "Omaha." Wallace LaFortune collection.

When it began in 1905 (Top), the Mitchell Bottling Works employees scrubbed bottles by hand and capped them with a pedal-operated machine at the rate of six per minute. The firm evolved into the Coca-Cola Bottling Company of Central South Dakota (Bottom). The building at the right was the old Holy Family Catholic Church which was moved to the South Kimball Street location where it eventually was converted into an apartment house and finally razed. Coca-Cola Bottling Company collection.

The merchants of yesteryear lacked electronic cash registers, checkout stands and other sophisticated refinements, but they made up for it with personal service to a clientele they generally knew on a first name basis. Shown here were the Mark Betts' mercantile in Mount Vernon (opposite page, bottom), the Reierson grocery in Mitchell (opposite page, top) and John and Julia Musil's general store in Ethan (above). Florence Althen, Roberta McEntee and Don Musil collections.

St. Joseph's Hospital was completed in 1906 at Fifth Avenue and Kittredge Street in Mitchell. Three months later a nursing school was established. The nurses pictured here were from a World War I era class. Queen of Peace Hospital archives.

Founded by the Presentation Sisters of Aberdeen, St. Joseph Hospital had a Catholic orientation for more than eight decades before it joined with the cross-town Methodist Hospital to form the ecumenical Queen of Peace medical center. Queen of Peace Hospital archives.

LEIGHTON SUPPLY CO.
UNITED
LEAD COMPANY
SAINT PAUL
CENTRAL SUPPLY CO.

The offices of Anderson's Lumber Yard (above) and Giese's sheet metal company (opposite page) may have been lacking in luxury, but later-day antique collectors would no doubt pay dearly for the rocking chairs and roll-top desk. Mitchell Area Historical Society and Donna Giese collections.

SUNSHINE BISCUITS
Takhoma Biscuit
Sunshine Biscuits

CHAPTER 7

The War to End All Wars— and the Tinsel Twenties

Mount Vernon didn't have a Corn Palace, but for three decades its Old Settlers' Day was the highlight of the town's year. People came by train, horse and buggy and finally the first sputtering automobiles to enjoy the gala celebrations. There were band concerts, shooting matches, greased pig chases, literary recitations, baseball games, parades, speeches, fireworks and a grand ball at the Opera House.

Races of all kinds were held: foot races, sack races, bicycle races and especially horse races. For a time, four-horse chariot races were featured. In 1904 Ezra Bailey and Clate Ink competed with four mules. A year earlier a balloon ascension captivated the crowd, but probably the most memorable event in the history of the annual affair was a Wild West show sponsored by Dr. Thomas B. Smiley. The shooting of the horse-stealing villain was so realistic, old-timers recalled, that ladies actually fainted at the sight of the fake blood.

Old Settlers' Day also brought back a flood of memories for the survivors of Davison County's beginnings, and at the same time it was symbolic of the advances made since the earlier settlements at Firesteel, Arlandton and Rome. When the 1917 event was cancelled, however, it brought to an end a relatively carefree era for South Dakotans far removed from international concerns.

On March 9, 1916, Francisco (Pancho) Villa had led a force of Mexican irregulars across the border in an attack on Columbus, New Mexico, killing 17 Americans. As a result, President Woodrow Wilson mobilized the South Dakota National Guard, including Company F of the Fourth South Dakota Infantry at Mitchell. Under the command of Captain Earl B. Rowley, the unit was sent to San Benito, Texas, to guard against any further incursions by Villa. When the organization returned some nine months months later, a giant civic welcoming party was staged. Mothers, wives and sweethearts relaxed with their men home again, but their relief was short-lived as a second call-up came in July of 1917 following the declaration of war against Germany on April 6.

This time the mobilization included Troop E of the Fourth South Dakota Cavalry which had been organized in Mitchell the previous

(Opposite page) Art and Oscar Reierson opened their first bakery in 1912, later expanding into the ice cream and grocery business. Their store was a showcase of imaginative display rivaling the decorations of the Corn Palace. Before the advent of refrigerated trucks, they used ice-cooled vans to deliver their Kreme Krust Bread and other products well beyond Davison County. Roberta McEntee collection.

October. Notre Dame Academy, the Catholic School which had been established in 1912, was turned over to the troops as a temporary barracks until they were shipped out. The men of Company F were billeted in the city hall auditorium where cots were removed occasionally to hold dances for morale purposes. When measles broke out in the unit, it was quarantined at the old Driving Park east of the city.

Finally, in September during Corn Palace Week, Company F was sent off amid the cheers of thousands to Camp Greene, North Carolina, to prepare for shipment to France. Troop E was assigned to Camp Cody near Deming, New Mexico, before it, too, was ordered overseas. Tragically, Pvt. Howard Barton fell ill and couldn't accompany his comrades, and shortly thereafter he became the first Davison County soldier to die in World War I service.

Meanwhile, the first draft registration was held on June 5, 1917, and a Davison County exemption board was created under the chairmanship of W. E. Tipton. Eventually more than 700 county men were in uniform, as well as eleven nurses, including Edna Walker and Bethilda Olson who served in France.

Space does not allow the relating of the deeds and deaths of all the Davison County men and women in service, but a few can be mentioned. Pfc. Harold Goodwin of Mitchell was cited for bravery with the Marines at Chateau Thierry where he was temporarily blinded in a gas attack. Pvt. Howard R. Dean, another Mitchell

The Erion Packing Company, which featured Custer Brand hams and bacon, was one of the many industries which flourished and then faded on the Mitchell scene. Mitchell Area Historical Society/Harry B. Hersey photo.

Company F of the Fourth South Dakota Infantry served on the Mexican border in 1916 and was recalled for active duty for World War I the following year. Before being sent to Camp Cody, New Mexico, enroute to overseas shipment, the unit was billeted in the Mitchell City Hall auditorium. Mitchell Area Historical Society/ Harry B. Hersey photo.

Marine, was wounded at Belleau Wood but was saved from death when a card case and Bible in his pocket deflected a jagged piece of shrapnel. Back in action, his rifle was shot out of his hands with no injury to him. Vincent Pollard of Mount Vernon, a messenger, escaped unharmed when the motorcycle he was riding was blown up under him.

Undoubtedly the most heroic of them all was Father Colman O'Flaherty, a military chaplain and former pastor of the Holy Family parish in Mitchell, who roamed the battlefields fearlessly, administering to wounded doughboys with no thought of exploding shells around him. On October 3, 1918, a few short weeks before the Armistice, he was killed by an artillery burst when he dashed out of a cellar against orders to kneel beside occupants of an ammunition truck which had been blown to bits. He was awarded the Distinguished Service Cross posthumously.

Back home Company I of the South Dakota Home Guard was organized to patrol Mitchell's railroads and warehouse district and to protect the town from the International Workers of the World, the dreaded "Wobblies." Mount Vernon hired a night watchman to make sure saboteurs didn't destroy the elevators. At Dakota Wesleyan 89 men enrolled in the Students' Army Training Corps as the basement of Science Hall and other campus buildings were turned into military barracks. Doctors Byron Bobb, William R. Ball, Floyd D. Gillis and William A. Delaney, Sr., were among those who volunteered

The Mitchell Kiwanis Club was chartered in 1921 with 118 members. The organization promoted the Custer Battlefield Highway (U. S. 16) in an industrial parade during the 1929 American Legion state convention in the Corn Palace City. Mitchell Area Historical Society/ Harry B. Hersey photo.

for military service, filling a need but putting extra pressure on physicians and nurses who remained behind and battled an influenza epidemic during and after the war. Incidentally, more Davison County men died of meningitis, flu, pneumonia and other diseases than were killed in action.

Mitchell got its second major health-care facility during the war when the Methodist Hospital was dedicated on February 10, 1918. A school of nursing, similar to the one established earlier at St. Joseph's Hospital, accepted its first "probationers" in April. Applicants for the course received the following instructions:

Please bring three striped gingham dresses . . . one-piece garments shirtwaist style, five inches from the floor . . . one half dozen aprons, plain . . . plenty of underclothing, all marked with the owner's name in indelible ink . . . two laundry bags, scissors, napkin ring and watch. Wear black shoes with rubber heels, white for summer. Hair to be plain but neat. No jewelry.

A spirit of patriotism ran high throughout the county. Davison citizens purchased more than two million dollars' worth of Liberty

Bonds during four loan drives. Mrs. W. S. Hill headed the food committee with chairmen in each township to promote meatless and wheatless days and other conservation measures. Restaurants and hotels were not allowed to serve sugar except on special request, and the availability of white bread was curtailed. A businessmen's brigade was formed to help in the harvest fields, and the Mitchell Chamber of Commerce promoted the planting of potatoes in "every available piece of ground in the city." The Milwaukee Road gave what it called a "substantial raise" to its workers, up from 17 1/2 cents to 20 cents. Men in the coal shed got an extra nickel, and all employees were permitted to plant vegetables in the railroad right-of-way.

There was strong anti-German sentiment throughout the state. German books and dishes were destroyed, and anyone who spoke the language of the enemy was considered traitorous. Those who didn't don a uniform, buy bonds, contribute to the Red Cross, work to produce food, send cigarettes to the boys or otherwise become involved in the war effort were branded as "slackers" and in some cases had their houses daubed with yellow paint.

Finally, on November 11, 1918, the "war to end all wars" came to an end. Although many of the original members of Company F and Troop E had been reassigned and scattered throughout other units, the remnants of the Davison County contingent returned home to an emotional reunion party. Then, despite the fact that there were gold stars in a few windows and some lives and businesses were severely disrupted, at least a semblance of normalcy was soon restored.

The Tinsel Twenties which followed brought changes unlike any in America's past. Grain prices dropped drastically from wartime highs and some farm bankruptcies resulted. National prohibition was imposed by the 18th Amendment, and the Mitchell Rotary Club—founded in 1917—held a mock funeral for John Barleycorn. The restrictive measure was supposed to produce a sober citizenry, but almost the opposite occurred as the era of flappers, bathtub gin, speakeasies and an uninhibited dance called the Charleston replaced the seriousness of the world conflict.

Davison County had its share of bootleggers to bedevil law enforcement officials who made occasional arrests and sometimes looked the other way. A booze-peddler from Huron was caught with 20 gallons of hootch and his Hudson car confiscated. Sheriff William W. Coons became a minor culprit himself when he was fined $50 for personally keeping almost half of the 700 pounds of sugar taken in a raid on a still near Mount Vernon. All in all, it was a decade mixed with frivolity, some economic nervousness and a generous portion of hope.

Old Settlers' Day was Mount Vernon's annual celebration, with parades, carnivals and even greased pig chases. The photographer's note on this picture of the 1914 event indicated that the band-led procession was a "march to the races" held at the edge of town. Mitchell Area Historical Society.

The town band was a regular participant in Mount Vernon's annual Old Settlers' Day which began in the 1880s and ended with World War I. Florence Althen collection.

The railroads were still a dominant factor in Davison County, although the Milwaukee Road suffered a serious loss when its roundhouse was destroyed on September 5, 1916. Two men were killed and five others injured when an acetylene gas welder exploded, blasting the roof off of eight stalls where engines were being repaired and shattering windows as far as two blocks away. *The Daily Republican* said the solid brick walls "crumbled like paper." Fortunately, the detonation occurred at 7:55 a.m. just before there would have been considerably more employees in the vicinity of the acetylene tank. The tracks were quickly cleared and reconstruction began almost immediately because of the importance of the building, the only maintenance point in the district where major overhauls could be made.

Meanwhile, town streets and country lanes were being churned up by Whippets, Maxwells, Jordans, Overlands, Saxons and—until he stopped making them in 1927—Henry Ford's ubiquitous Model T's. Airplanes, no longer an uncommon sight, landed in county pastures, while throughout the United States Charles A. Lindbergh was the hero of the day after he and his "Spirit of St. Louis" flew across the Atlantic Ocean in May of 1927. Later that summer he made a barnstorming trip to South Dakota, and Mitchellites were eagerly hopeful that he would choose their town for one of his few stops. On August 27 most of the rooftops were covered with people anxious to get a glimpse of Lindy's plane. According to eye-witnesses, it was a thrilling sight, but everyone was keenly disappointed when they learned that he wasn't going to land. Instead, at 11:05 a.m., he merely flew over the city and dropped a message which fell to the ground at the corner of Third Avenue and Main Street. *The Evening Republican* reported that the scroll was picked up by 13-year-

(Above) The Gale Theatre, built in 1906, is shown in its hey-day, with vaudeville and pictures on its bill. (Opposite page) The theatre burned on March 26, 1914. Fighting the fire was complicated by the fact that the water hydrants were frozen. Mitchell Area Historical Society.

old Leo McIntyre, and the "Lone Eagle's" greeting—which included a plug for airmail and commercial aviation—was posted in the window of the Nicolls-Kress Pharmacy for all to see.

In Ethan the late 1920s brought a much needed industry. A cheese factory began operation on June 27, 1928, and had an almost immediate positive effect on the town and surrounding country. Farmers, instead of selling out, added to their dairy herds and received top prices for milk and sweet cream. Hog production increased with whey from the cheese plant as a feed supplement. The *Ethan Enterprise* reported that the Improved Sausage Company, which had moved to Ethan from Mitchell, was doing a rushing business, an active poultry market had developed and the three elevators were prospering.

Of considerable excitement in Mitchell was the advent of talking pictures. In 1928 the Metropolitan Theatre (which had replaced the old Gale Theatre after it burned on March 26, 1914) began showing "fully synchronized" movies with titles like "The Lion and the Mouse," "State Street Sadie" and "The Whip," a horse racing story. In September of 1929, the Met, as the movie house was familiarly known, presented "The Jazz Singer" starring Al Jolson, the historic full-length feature which changed the cinema industry. It also signalled the end of work for the pit orchestra at the Met and the piano player at the Lyric, then Mitchell's other theater.

If Davison County had any natural shortcomings, it was the lack of any noteworthy geographic features. The terrain was primarily rolling prairie with no mountains, gorges or sylvan lakes. The valley and bluffs of the Jim River in Perry and Mitchell Townships added a bit of character to the land in the northeast corner of the county, while Firesteel Creek, Enemy Creek, Twelve Mile Creek and Morris Run provided west-to-east drainage through lesser vales and draws.

Potable water for farms and towns came mostly from wells—some shallow, some deep artesian flows—but as Mitchell grew in population, the city's needs increased greatly.

The concept of creating an artificial lake by damming Firesteel Creek apparently was considered on several occasions through the years, and in 1927 a bond issue of $350,000 was finally approved to move ahead on the project. The farm land of various owners—including John, Joe and Charlie Anderson, Nels Jensen, George Atkinson and others—was acquired on the north edge of the city, and horse-drawn scrapers began scooping out the basin. A concrete dam was completed in 1928, and in March of the following year the water level in Lake Mitchell had risen high enough to flow over the spillway. It was man-made, of course, but the 600-acre lake with a watershed of more than 500 square miles at last gave Davison County its own unique recreational area as well as a dependable source of water for the county seat.

A half year later—on October 29, 1929—Black Friday brought panic to Wall Street. The sudden collapse of the stock market half a continent away, coupled with the afflictions of nature which followed, signalled the beginning of the Great Depression, an era to be forever remembered in South Dakota and throughout mid-America as the Dirty Thirties.

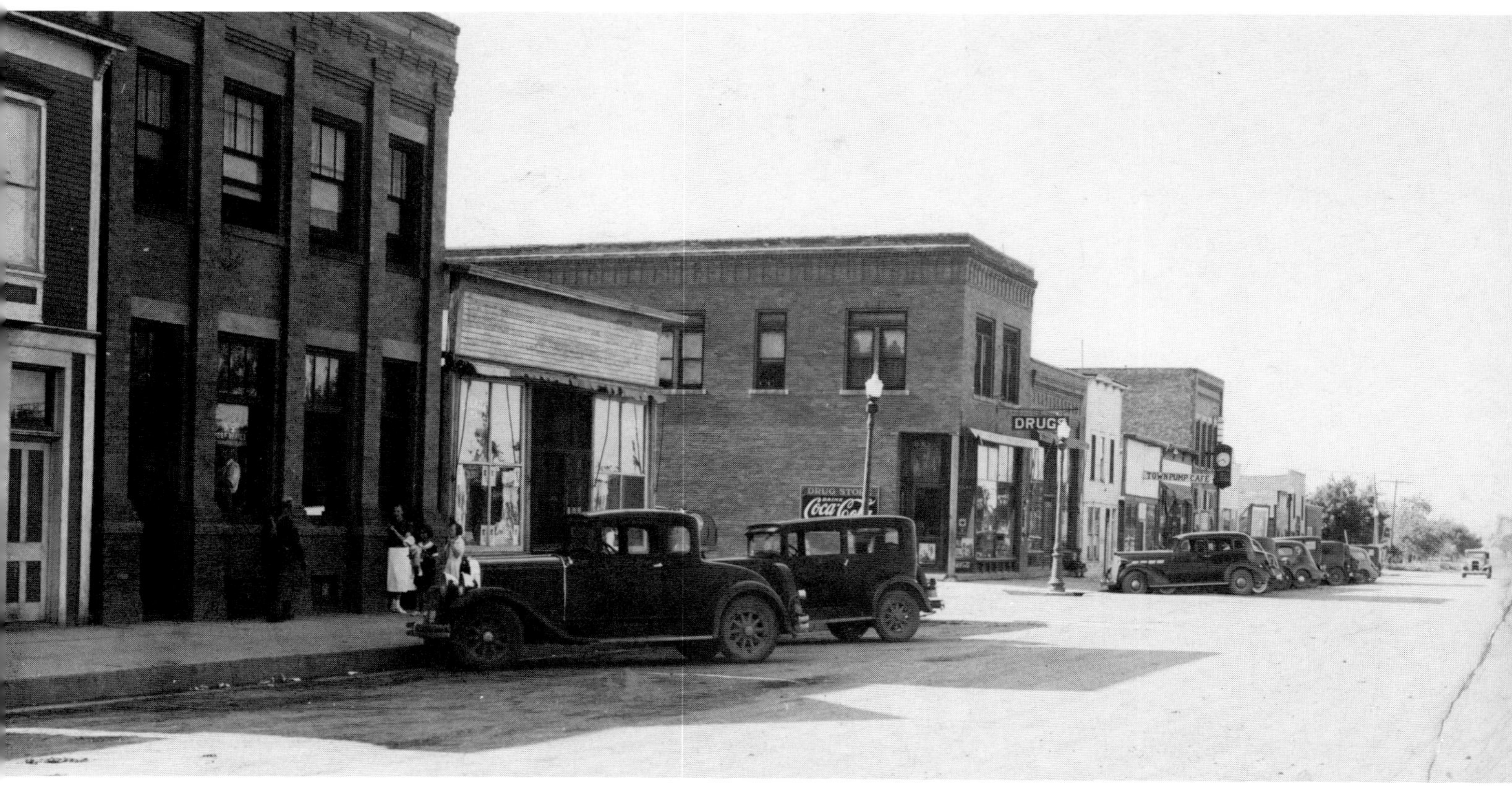

Mount Vernon's Main Street—typical of South Dakota towns of its size—changed considerably with the passage of time: from dirt surface to paving, from horses to automobiles. (Top) Mount Vernon Library; (bottom) Wally and Billie Zeal collection.

The men of Mitchell got their morning shave at the Central Barber Shop on Main Street in 1916. It was almost a ritualistic process, topped off by a hot towel treatment. Mitchell Area Historical Society.

Among the floats in the 1924 harvest festival parade in Ethan was one featuring the ladies of the Royal Neighbors of America with a patriotic theme. Parades were a continuing form of diversion almost from the beginning of Davison County's history. Vern and Tracy Wittstruck collection.

A. J. "Tony" Rozum came to Mitchell as chief dispatcher for the Milwaukee Road before opening his Ford automobile dealership in 1917. The firm survived the Dirty Thirties by taking grain in trade for cars. In addition to grain bins, the basement of the original building had been used as a dance hall, bowling alley and miniature golf course. Rozum Motors collection.

An explosion which was heard two miles away literally demolished the Milwaukee Road's roundhouse and shops in Mitchell on September 5, 1916. The facility employed as many as 200 men and was an important factor in the city's economy. Mitchell Area Historical Society.

The Mitchell Country Club was organized by golf enthusiasts on June 28, 1915. It was the era of sand greens, when men wore knickers, and clubs were known, not by numbers, but as niblicks, cleeks, mashies and midirons. J. Leonard Jennewein photo collection with the N. J. Dunham manuscript, Layne Library, Dakota Wesleyan.

The Methodist State Hospital (as it was originally named) was dedicated on February 10, 1918. The "State" was later dropped to avoid misinterpretation that the facility was government-operated or a mental institution. Tuberculosis patients were cared for in the building extension at left. Mitchell Area Historical Society/Harry B. Hersey photo.

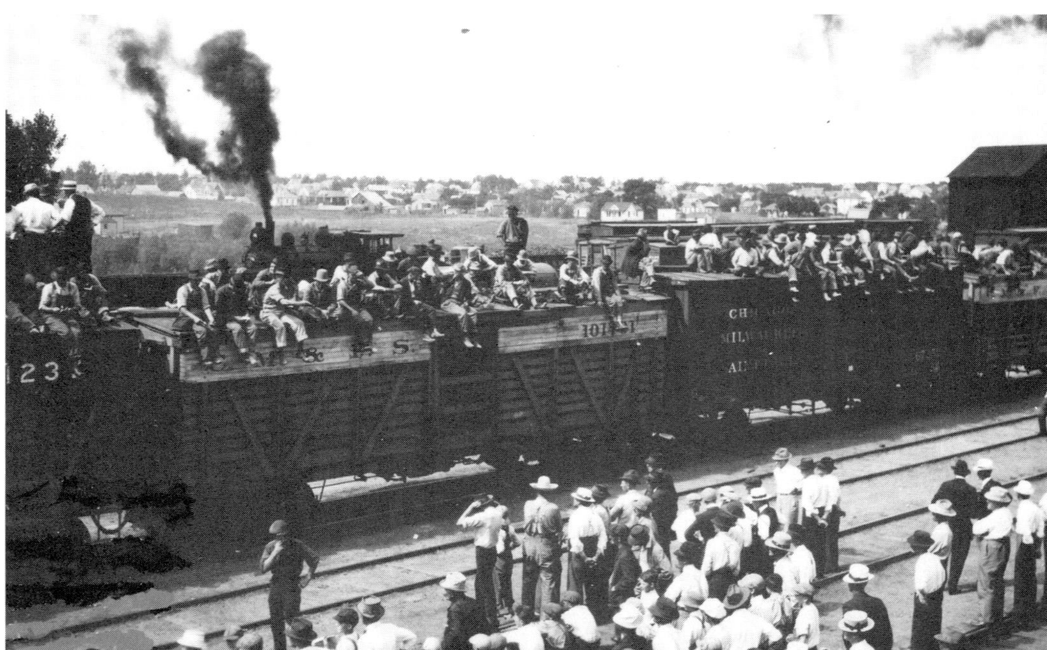

Members of the Industrial Workers of the World (the I.W.W. "wobblies") faced confrontation when they passed through Mitchell on a Milwaukee Road freight train in 1916. They were reputedly communists even before the Russian revolution and were considered a radical element in the U. S. during the World War I era. Pat Briedenbach collection/ Harry B. Hersey photo.

The Isaac Spears Ice Company provided door-to-door service to customers in Mitchell before the advent of the refrigerator. The firm's ice storage houses eventually were destroyed by a fire believed to have been started by young boys smoking cigarettes. Ralph Boone collection.

Lakeshore Drive across the Lake Mitchell dam boasted a paved surface when most of the other area roads were still graveled. The dam was completed in 1928 and the lake level rose high enough to go over the spillway the following year. Mitchell Area Historical Society and William Timmins collections.

By comparison with other areas of South Dakota, Davison County lacks geographic diversity. However, several small streams—like Twelve Mile Creek, at right—drain the rolling prairies from west to east into the Jim River. Leo and Sally Pollreisz collection.

Mayor Tom Ball drove the symbolic first spike for the Mitchell Street and Interurban Railroad on August 25, 1915. The brainchild of Oscar E. "Squire" Cassem, a land-developer, it began at West First and Rowley, connected the Milwaukee and Omaha depots and then extended farther north, hopefully to create a market for some of Cassem's land. It lasted less than three years. Edna Weller collection/ L. E. Stair photo.

Lake Mitchell was formed when Firesteel Creek was dammed in 1928. It quickly became a favorite all-season recreational area for the entire county and a dependable source of water for the city. When filled to the top of the spillway, it was more than forty feet deep in some places. Mitchell Area Historical Society.

1929

Stair
Artist

The Rozum Motor Company of Mitchell provided the "modern" equipment to meet the food demands of World War I. It was a boom time for farmers as even marginal land was tilled. However, following the Armistice, prices dropped drastically during the "return to normalcy." Ole Leeland photo.

Tom McComish's butcher shop at 113 East Third in Mitchell was typical of the meat markets of the post-World War I era. Mitchell Area Historical Society.

(Opposite page) Photographer Lawrence E. Stair obviously posed these employees of the Mitchell Steam Laundry shortly after the turn of the century because it is unlikely that they normally worked in such Sunday-go-to-meeting attire. Mitchell Area Historical Society.

J. F. ANDER
LUMBER

Because of its railroad connections, Mitchell developed a warehouse district and became a distribution center for Davison and surrounding counties. The Haley and Lang firm (inset above) preceded the Haley Neeley Wholesale Fruit Company (large photo). Mitchell Area Historical Society and William Timmins collections.

When horses were replaced by automobiles and motorized farm equipment, the petroleum industry became an important economic factor. National Refining Company trucks (top) delivered White Rose gas to farm customers, while numerous service stations preceded the later-day U-pump facilities. Garnet Folkerts and Dr. Richard I. Porter collections.

Henry Stopfer and William Hohn (second and third from the left) operated a popular saloon in Ethan in pre-World War I days. Women rarely entered such establishments then, but there were chairs behind the building and a parking area for horses and buggies where wives and girlfriends could be served or just wait for their husbands and beaus. Mitchell Area Historical Society.

LYRIC
LYRIC
The Latest Features, Comedies & News
SYNCHRONIZED ON THE AUDITONE
PRICES 10 & 25
CONTINUOUS SHOWING 2:30 TO 11 P.M. DAILY
COFFEE CUP LUNCH
C.W. ADAMS TAILOR
SERVED AT ALL HOURS
NAVIN
CAFE
Green Lantern

CHAPTER 8

Drouth, Debt, and Destruction

Davison County did not immediately feel the effects of the stock market crash, but by the time President Franklin Delano Roosevelt took office in 1933, the Great Depression had reached South Dakota in full fury. With it came the dust storms, grasshoppers, searing summer heat and anthrax, a killing livestock disease which could also infect humans.

Before and during the economic doldrums of the thirties, two banks each in Ethan and Mount Vernon closed their doors, as did five out of seven in Mitchell. Across the state depositors lost some \$39 million as the result of the failures. Farm prices dropped to disastrous levels. "Shelled corn was selling for two cents a bushel and ear corn for three cents less" was the way one observer described it. Farmers shipped hogs to market and didn't receive enough to pay the trucking costs. In a sand pit west of Ethan 400 head of diseased cattle were shot and buried.

As powder-fine top soil piled up along fencelines, farm closures followed, and tens of thousands disheartened South Dakotans joined the out-migration from the Dust Bowl of middle America. Davison County's population decreased from 16,821 in 1930 to 15,336 in 1940. That may not sound like a serious loss, but many of those who remained were clinging to fiscal straws. By 1934 almost 40 percent of the state's people were on relief rolls, the highest ratio in any of the 48 states.

Years later many of the tenacious survivors would say: "We didn't know we were poor because most everyone else was in the same boat." As the "black blizzards" continued, nurses at the Methodist Hospital soaked sheets in water and hung them over the windows to keep out the dust. Farmers spread poisoned grain to control the grasshoppers; they also poured molasses over Russians thistles and other weedy forage to keep cattle alive. Somehow self-help, neighborliness and Franklin Roosevelt's New Deal managed to overcome the worst effects of the disaster.

(Opposite page) In the 1930s the Lyric Theatre offered continuous showings from 2:30 to 11:00 p.m. at ten and twenty-five cents admission. It, the Coffee Cup and Green Lantern Cafes as well as the Navin Hotel all became victim of the changing times. C. W. Adams offered tailor-made suits for \$29.50 in the Coffee Cup building. Mitchell Area Historical Society.

Of special note must be the work of William Roy Ronald, who had come from the *Sioux Falls Press* to buy the *Mitchell Daily Republican* and who was to become a strong voice in South Dakota journalism until his death in 1951. Through the years his editorial policy had reflected his progressive Republican beliefs, but when the Depression hit and he saw the plight of the farmers, he endorsed

Roosevelt's candidacy. As a result, he was offered an important position by Secretary of Agriculture Henry Wallace (which he declined), but he was credited with authoring a substantial portion of the Agricultural Adjustment Act, the New Deal's Triple A. At home he met considerable opposition from his conservative friends which he countered with an unusual gesture. Old-time members of his newspaper staff recalled how he walked into the composing room in 1934, took a hacksaw and cut the "an" off the *Republican*. After that the paper became the less politically labeled *Daily Republic*.

Fortunately, to match the drastic loss of income, prices for food, clothing and other commodities also dropped. Steve Ptak's grocery store in Mitchell sold milk for six cents a quart, three dozen eggs for a quarter and a porkchop for just a penny. The shoe store started by John Burg in 1910 was one of the firms which accepted chickens and eggs in lieu of cash. The Rozum Motor Company established in 1917 by A. J. (Tony) Rozum traded vehicles and farm machinery for grain which was stored in bins in the basement. Survival became more important than profits.

To maintain morale, an emphasis was placed on free or lowcost recreation and entertainment. Baseball and softball leagues flourished, and movies offered a brief escape from reality. Flickering films were shown in the old Odd Fellows Hall in Mount Vernon before Roy Brown converted the building into a farm service store; and for

Local residents and Mitchell visitors didn't understand a welcome party for someone called "Uncle Joe" on October 3, 1931. It was staged by entertainers at the Corn Palace as an expression of affection for Joe Bren, head of the theatrical department of the talent-booking agency, the Music Corporation of America. The 147th Field Artillery Band, with a long history in Mitchell, joined the depot reception. Mitchell Area HistoricalSociety/Harry B. Hersey photo.

fifteen cents you could enjoy talkies in Ethan at Fred Weepie's Hall where merchants sponsored a drawing for $10, plus free entertainment, as a trade stimulator on Saturday nights.

In Mitchell the aging Met Theatre became the Paramount; the unventilated Lyric closed and was succeeded by the air-conditioned Time in the Medical Arts Building. With construction work at a virtual stand-still in California, contractor Nelson Logan returned to Mitchell to assist his ailing father in the latter's real estate ventures. That's when the younger Logan established the Roxy Theatre in the former Western Chevrolet Company building where John J. Verschoor, who founded the firm in 1926, had also sold Whippets, Flints, Hupmobiles, Auburns and Cords.

Logan was an imaginative promoter. He paid workmen with his corporation's stock which in turn was accepted in trade by at least one Mitchell store. Instead of the traditional male ushers, he hired

Davison County benefitted from the New Deal's Works Progress Administration in the form of roads, dams and public buildings. The W.P.A. also sponsored writing, art and recreational activities, including such intensely serious competitions like marble tournaments. Mitchell Area Historical Society.

pretty girls for the job. While theaters elsewhere offered simple bank night drawings, Logan called his lottery "Pirate Night" and dressed his young usherettes in short-skirted buccaneer costumes complete with wooden swords. For a time he even exhibited monkeys and a lion named "Duke" to attract viewers.

He also put a beacon light on a 50-foot tower atop his theater. It had another purpose besides calling attention to his enterprise, though. As a pilot who had served in the Army Air Corps during World War I, he was concerned about night fliers getting lost with nothing to lead them to Mitchell's airport. His revolving searchlight—which could be seen for 30 miles on a clear night—could guide them to the town which they could then circle until local autoists assembled at the airfield to permit a safe landing with the beams from their headlights.

Whether or not his Roxy tower was thus utilized, aviation had definitely arrived in Davison County. In May of 1938 Malcolm B. Ronald, who would later succeed his father as publisher of the *Daily Republic*, made the first airmail flight from Mitchell to Huron with a 34-pound bag of letters. Before that, though, he flew through threatening weather to Ethan, where he landed in a pasture, and to Mount Vernon, where the airport was an alfalfa patch, gathering up the mail

The Louis Beckwith house in the background of this parade photo became the centerpiece of the Friends of the Middle Border Museum. It was moved to the museum complex adjacent to the Dakota Wesleyan campus and restored with period furnishings and decor. Mitchell Area Historical Society.

The Daily Republic staff of 1958 included longtime executive editor Ezra M. "Ez" Brady (third from right, back row). Beginning in 1931 as an 18-year-old cub reporter, he rose through the ranks to become a journalistic legend in his own time. As a young sports editor, he once got into an editorial feud with a Yankton College student reporter known as "Penny" Nichol. Years later he and Federal Judge Fred Nichol became good friends. Irma Helgeland collection.

at each stop to add to his pouch before his historic 37-minute trip to the Beadle County seat. Two years later Ronald became director of a Civilian Pilot Training Program for which fifteen Dakota Wesleyan students qualified. Nationally it prepared thousands of fliers for the yet unknown war emergency. Ronald also is credited with being a founder of Alcoholics Anonymous in Mitchell.

For others, Lake Mitchell became a favored spot "to get away from it all." People from throughout the region were invited to "Lake Mitchell Day" for free fishing, free lemonade, free lunch, free golf, free swimming and a free band concert. The price was certainly right, and anglers were allowed a limit of ten bullheads, crappies or sunfish—and all the carp, buffalo, suckers and red horse they could catch. Meanwhile, the annual Corn Palace celebration was held, although because of the drouth, only a few bushels of colored corn were available for decorations in 1931 and evergreen boughs were brought from the Black Hills to supplement the meager supply of grain. The bands of Lou Breese, Frankie Masters, Herbie Kay and Isham Jones were among the featured entertainers during the depression era.

One of the most visible of the New Deal initial programs was the Works Progress Administration. In Mitchell the W.P.A. financed a

Pirate Night at the Roxy Theatre drew a large crowd in 1935 when the weekly cash prize had risen to $400, a considerable sum in depression days. Buyers of absentee tickets could wait outside where the winning name was announced over loudspeakers. Jeff Logan collection/Harry B. Hersey photo.

community recreation center and a new county courthouse. The latter's primary designer was Floyd F. Kings, son of Andrew Kings, the long-time city councilman and school board member who had built the first Corn Palace, the First National Bank, College Hall at Dakota Wesleyan, Central High School, the Holy Family Catholic Church, the original Elks' Lodge, the Carnegie Library and numerous other buildings in eastern South Dakota. The younger Kings decorated the balustrades of the courthouse with figures of wheat sheaves and grasshoppers as symbolic of the times. They were later sandblasted off because of the negative connotation of the 'hoppers.

The W.P.A. also was involved in improvements to the school athletic field. In 1940 the wooden football grandstand dating back to 1929 burned down after the high school's homecoming game on Friday night. Investigators believed the cause was a carelessly thrown cigarette. On the following Saturday Dakota Wesleyan had its Blue and White Day, and spectators had to bring chairs or stand for the game. The school district then shared costs with the W.P.A. for the erection of a new concrete stadium with dressing rooms and shower facilities. Earlier the Mitchell Baseball Association worked with the New Deal program to build a grandstand and a first-class playing field.

Oscar Howe, a Yanktonai Sioux and a graduate of Dakota Wesleyan, was commissioned by the government program to paint a mural with an Indian motif on the interior of the Mitchell library's dome. The building, incidentally, had been made possible by a $10,000 grant from steel magnate Andrew Carnegie and was erected in 1902. Seventy years later it was leased to the Mitchell Area Arts Council for a dollar a year after a new public library had been built. The old Carnegie later became the Oscar Howe Art Center. In addition to supporting art projects, the W.P.A., at one of its work center in Mitchell, contracted with unemployed writers to produce numerous publications, including *South Dakota Place Names*, an important reference work.

In Mount Vernon—seemingly forever plagued by fires—the W. D. Anderson Mercantile Store burned to the ground in 1937. The land on which the store was located belonged to Bernice Brown Smiley, widow of Dr. Thomas Smiley who had purchased the building for his office and residence on the second floor when he first came to the town in 1896. (Incidentally, he shared space with Mount Vernon's first library, and his receptionist, Myrtle Bromwell, also served as a part-time librarian.) After the fire Mrs. Smiley deeded the lot to the town as the site for an auditorium which was built by W.P.A. workers.

In December of 1936 the state administrative office for the New Deal program was transferred from Pierre to Mitchell, a small retribution for the loss of the capital 32 years earlier. It remained in the Davison County seat until the final W.P.A. phase-out in 1943. Also in December of 1936, U.S. Senator Peter Norbeck died at age 66, and the naming of his successor took on a complicated political twist. It was thought that Democratic Governor Tom Berry would resign so he could be appointed to the vacancy, but Robert Peterson, the lieutenant governor, was under arrest for the alleged shortage of $170,000 from a Centerville bank. Next in line of succession was Myrtle Robinson, the secretary of state, who was in a Sioux City hospital recovering from surgery. Governor Berry finally solved the dilemma by naming Mitchell attorney Herbert E. Hitchcock of the historic Hitchcock

To promote the Roxy Theatre, Nelson Logan bought an African lion named "Duke" which he exhibited in a cage off the theatre lobby. He claimed it was captured by Frank "Bring 'em Back Alive" Buck, who came to see the lion and became one of Logan's good friends. Jeff Logan collection.

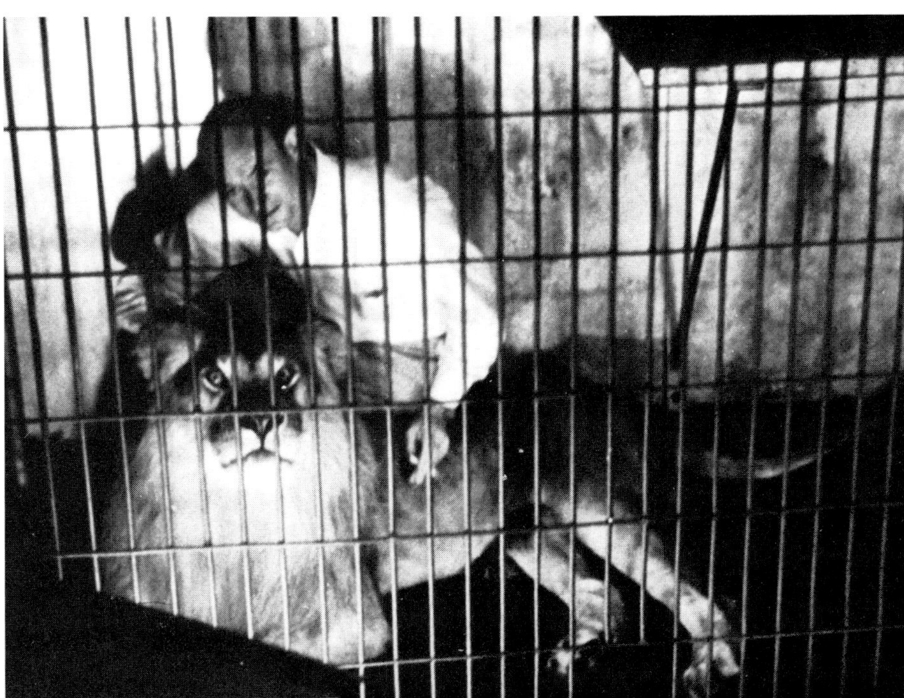

family to complete the remaining two years of Norbeck's term. Though he was succeeded by Gladys Pyle of Huron in the unusual "short term" election in 1938, he continued to be a prominent figure in Davison County affairs until his death in 1958 at age 90.

Eventually, of course, the depressing decade passed into history, but before it did, it saw the beginning of two very positive activities which would have continuing value to the county, both historically and from a tourism standpoint. The first was the incorporation of the Friends of the Middle Border on December 23, 1939, an association to preserve the heritage of a seven-state area, but especially that of South Dakota. It was principally the brainchild of Leland D. Case, a graduate of Dakota Wesleyan, and took its name from a term popularized in the writings of Hamlin Garland, one of the founders. Museum space was provided in Dakota Hall at D.W.U. where, tragically, a destructive fire on February 12, 1955, resulted in the loss of irreplaceable manuscripts, original art and other memorabilia. However, with new resolve the University built another Dakota Hall, and the museum was re-established in a separate complex on the campus where its collections and impact grew year by year.

The second development actually had its origins in prehistoric times. Early white settlers in Davison County had occasional contact with the Native Americans (mostly Lakota Sioux) of their era, but along Firesteel Creek—among later-day artifacts like arrowheads

In 1937 the Time Theatre on Mitchell's Main Street featured Jane Withers in "Angel's Holiday," while Nelson Logan's Roxy competed for attention with a rooftop promotional sign over the Corner Drug Store. State Highway 37 then ran through the center of town, taking traffic past the Corn Palace. Clyde Goin collection.

and buffalo bone implements—were evidences of an earlier people. Little was done about the strange indentations in the earth near the northern limits of Mitchell until 1922 when W. H. Over, curator of the museum which was to bear his name at the University of South Dakota, mapped the site and counted 45 possible locations of ancient dwellings.

The C.M.&St.P. depot in Mitchell was a bustling place during the heyday of railroading. The arrival of the coast-to-coast Columbian Flier in 1931 was a notable event (bottom). The baggage department handled daily shipments of almost every conceivable commodity, including cream and baby chicks (top). Mitchell Area Historical Society/L. E. Stair photo; (bottom) J. Leonard Jennewein photo collection with the N. J. Dunham manuscript, Layne Library, Dakota Wesleyan University.

Only casual interest was shown in the findings for another 16 years until 1938 when Over, a representative of the Smithsonian Institution and members of the Mitchell Lions Club excavated two of the sites with the aid of a W.P.A. grant. They found remnants of an extinct culture, and the Lions Club rebuilt one hut with limited knowledge and materials thought to be similar to those used in the original construction. It turned out to be a futile gesture because vandals eventually destroyed their work. In ensuing years students from Dakota Wesleyan and the University of Wisconsin made exploratory excavations, but no continuing, organized effort was pursued until 1972 when the Mitchell Chamber of Commerce hired Darrell Fulmer as a resident archaeologist to begin an on-going program of study and restoration.

What evolved was the Mitchell Prehistoric Indian Village which

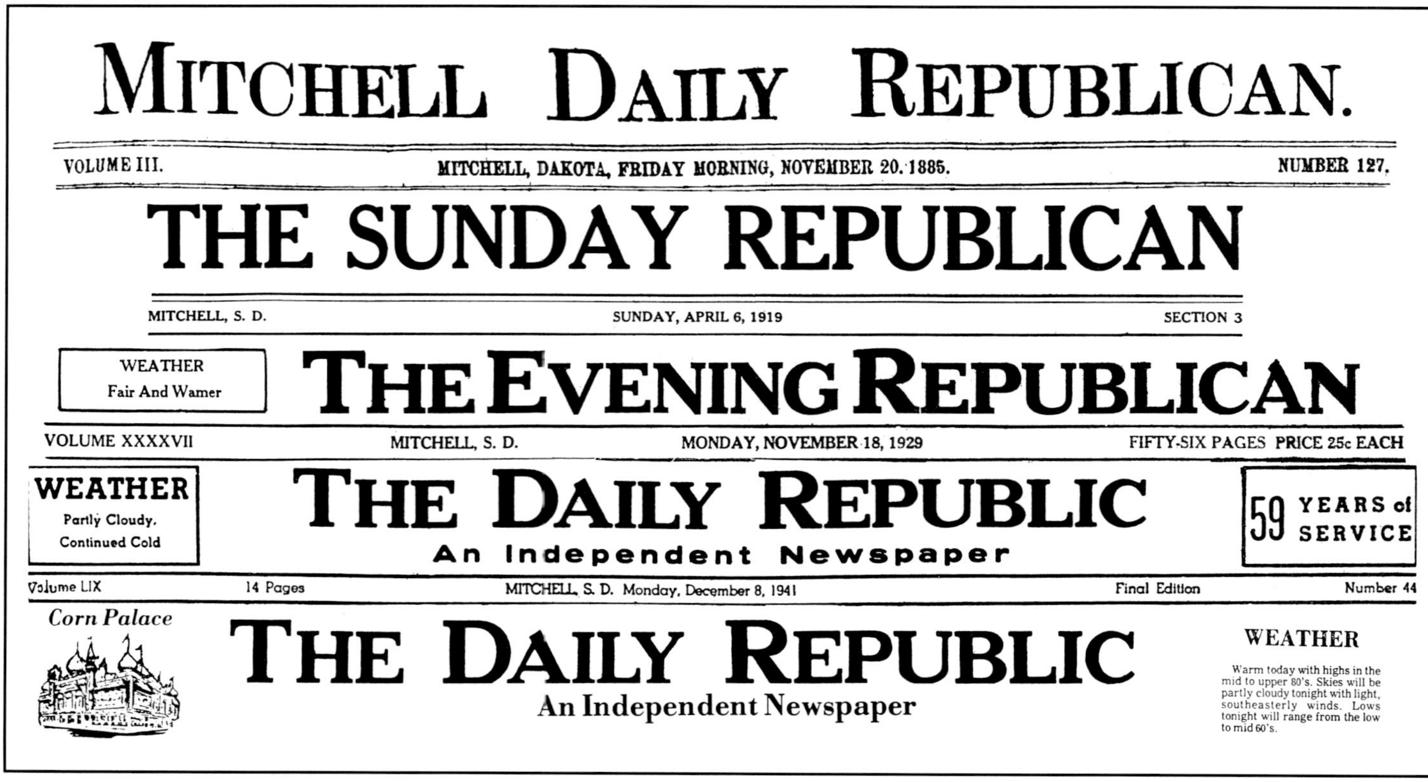

MITCHELL DAILY REPUBLICAN.

VOLUME III. MITCHELL, DAKOTA, FRIDAY MORNING, NOVEMBER 20, 1885. NUMBER 127.

THE SUNDAY REPUBLICAN

MITCHELL, S. D. SUNDAY, APRIL 6, 1919 SECTION 3

WEATHER
Fair And Wamer

THE EVENING REPUBLICAN

VOLUME XXXXVII MITCHELL, S. D. MONDAY, NOVEMBER 18, 1929 FIFTY-SIX PAGES PRICE 25c EACH

WEATHER
Partly Cloudy.
Continued Cold

THE DAILY REPUBLIC
An Independent Newspaper

59 YEARS of SERVICE

Volume LIX 14 Pages MITCHELL, S. D. Monday, December 8, 1941 Final Edition Number 44

Corn Palace

THE DAILY REPUBLIC
An Independent Newspaper

WEATHER
Warm today with highs in the mid to upper 80's. Skies will be partly cloudy tonight with light, southeasterly winds. Lows tonight will range from the low to mid 60's.

The evolution of The Daily Republic *is traced in its changing nameplate. Established as a weekly in 1882, it became a daily in 1885. Throughout much of its existence, its editorial stance remained true to its* Republican *title. However, in 1934 publisher William R. Ronald supposed-ly removed the "an" with a hacksaw to permit a more independent policy.*

won recognition as a National Archaelogical Landmark. A museum named in honor of Leo J. and Elsie Boehnen was constructed as well as replicas of the living quarters of the residents whose true identity remains shrouded in mystery. It is thought that as many as a thousand non-nomadic farmer-hunters may have lived in some 70 well-constructed dirt-floor lodges in their fortified enclave some ten centuries ago. Archaelogists are still asking the questions: Were they the ancestors of the Arikaras or Mandans? If so, where did they come from and where did they go?

Just when it appeared that a new and prosperous age was dawning, the United States found itself engulfed in World War II. However, more than a year before the bombing of Pearl Harbor by the Japanese on December 7, 1941, Davison County troops in the 147th Field Artillery Regiment of the National Guard were called to active duty. Members of the Mitchell-based Battery B, the regimental band and service platoon were on a train enroute to Fort Ord, California, with little more than a week to put their civilian affairs in order. For almost eleven months they were in training with other elements of the 147th until on November 22, 1941, they embarked on the *Willard A. Holbrook*, a converted liner, destined for the Philippine Islands.

Ironically, on November 27 they arrived at Pearl Harbor where they were given shore leave to enjoy the sights of Honolulu. Their convoy departed on the 30th, and a week later—when they were "somewhere in the Pacific"—they got the startling news that they had luckily avoided the debacle in Hawaii. New orders directed them to the Fiji Islands, and for many of them it marked the beginning of a war-time odyssey which would end only with final victory.

They, of course, were not the only Davison County men and women who would wear the uniform of the various services during the ensuing four years. One other National Guard unit—the Medical Detachment of the 109th Quartermaster Regiment, also with Mitchell as its home station—received an early call but was split up for duty in other organizations. Almost a thousand other individuals (precise statistics were never compiled) volunteered or were drafted to serve in scattered theatres around the globe. They participated in numerous acts of heroism—not all recorded—and too many made the supreme sacrifice.

From Davison County, as representative examples, Dr. John T. Smiley of Mount Vernon received the Legion of Merit for providing care of the sick and wounded in the North Burma campaign. Pfc. Harold L. Adams, twice wounded, was awarded both the Bronze and Silver Stars for his valorous conduct before an enemy pillbox near Zweibrucken, Germany, and for volunteering with a comrade to string a half mile of telephone wire under machine gun and small arms fire in France. Rear Admiral Lloyd J. Wiltse, son of the first Corn Palace photographer, was highly decorated for "extraordinary heroism" as a Navy task force commander in the Pacific, as was Army Air Corps pilot Robert F. McMahon who shot down three Japanese planes in one action near Darwin, Australia, before he was forced to bail out of his own blazing craft. McMahon's grandfather was Andrew J. Kings, the county's noted contractor.

Ethan named its new American Legion post after

The *Daily Republican* and *Weekly Capital* were published in the Mitchell Printing Company plant (top). The type was hand-set in the combination composing and press room (bottom). In 1901 a Simplex typesetting machine was purchased for $1,800, a giant stride toward modernization. Mitchell Area Historical Society.

Grandson of Andrew J. Kings, builder of the first Corn Palace, Army Air Corps pilot Robert F. McMahon was a decorated World War II ace, downing three Japanese planes in a single action. Mitchell Area Historical Society.

Alvin Erpenbach who was the victim of an enemy mine in Italy. The Mount Vernon post, originally honoring Pfc. McKinley Pound who died in the Meuse-Argonne offensive in World War I, added Dale V. Uhre, a sailor who was killed in action during the Guadalcanal campaign. At Post No. 18 in Mitchell the name of 19-year-old Herman A. Goetsch, a Pearl Harbor casualty, joined that of William H. Coacher who died of wounds in France in 1917. There was an ironic twist to Goetsch's death. The young seaman had run out of underwear during an illness and was wearing shorts stenciled with the name of a Mitchell buddy, William Hickey. The latter was listed as killed in action when Goetsch's body was first mistakenly identified by the borrowed shorts, and Hickey's mother received the dreaded War Department telegram ahead of a letter from her son announcing his safety.

Will G. Robinson, the state historian, spent four years assembling the best possible record of South Dakota's World War II casualties. In the end he admitted frustration because of inadequate reporting as he verified that at least 1,338 men from the state had been killed in action, were missing or otherwise died as the result of combat. His list included 35 from Davison County, among them Wilbert O. Wittenhagen, James L. Bailey, Wesley R. Doty, Vincent I. Taylor and Harold A. Gabriel. Louis and Francis Meyer of Mitchell both were killed in plane crashes and a third brother, Cletus, died in Australia, a triple blow to one family. How many died of disease or other causes during or after the war has never been determined.

On the home front the war affected everybody one way or another. Extensive rationing, bond drives, bandage wrapping, blackout drills, victory gardens and the knitting of olive drab and navy blue scarves became a shared responsibility of the all-out effort. The collection of scrap metal, kitchen fat, phonograph records, paper, rubber, tin cans and other materials necessary for military needs received the highest priority of patriotic citizens. Students and business people helped farmers harvest their crops, and school children in 36 counties east of the Missouri collected 14,000 bags of milkweed floss to provide insulation for pilots' jackets before a synthetic substance became available.

In Mitchell the Rozum Motor Company converted to war-time work, and its home shop and a branch factory in Watertown turned out small aircraft engine parts, precision dies, pouches and other critical material. Its work force included women, disabled men, World War I veterans and married fathers too old for military service. In 1941 the Mitchell Produce Company was cracking and drying thousands of eggs daily. At first the powdered eggs were allocated primarily to Great Britain, but they eventually ended up in military menus, too, not always to the delight of GIs.

Under the National Youth Administration—a lingering carry-over from the New Deal—training centers in Mitchell and Pierre administered shop units in other towns where young people, mostly from rural backgrounds—learned various mechanical skills while manufacturing products for the U.S. Arsenal at Rock Island, Illinois. (By 1943 most draft-age men not otherwise deferred, went directly into defense work or military service, so the program was discontinued.)

The Mitchell Municipal Airport north of the city had its alfalfa runways replaced with concrete, paid for by federal funds so that it could serve as a support facility for the Sioux City Army Air Base. Actor-turned-airman Jimmy Stewart was one of the pilots who flew into the Mitchell field which accommodated both B-17 and B-24 bombers. Although the number of servicemen at the Davison County installation was relatively small and kept a "military secret," a Mitchell Soldier Center—which never qualified for official U.S.O. designation—was established to provide dances, snacks, sewing services and other morale-boosting activities. County residents contributed almost sixty thousand dollars to the Red Cross, and the Ethan Commercial Club sponsored a rabbit hunt for Red Cross relief. Patriotic Davison

As if the depression and drought weren't enough, there was still another fire on Mitchell's Main Street on November 9, 1935, at Butterfield's Department Store. Mitchell Area Historical Society/Ole Leeland photo.

Charles and Mollie Kehler operated their popcorn stand at Third and Main in Mitchell. They were especially busy during Corn Palace week. J. Leonard Jennewein photo collection with the N. J. Dunham manuscript, Layne Library, Dakota Wesleyan University.

County citizens also bought more than ten million dollars in government bonds during the war years.

Then, finally, on May 6, 1945, Germany surrendered less than a month after the death of President Roosevelt. On August 6 President Harry Truman ordered the first of two atomic bombs dropped on Japan—and eight days later the long, costly conflict came to an abrupt close.

After V-J Day Davison County—like the rest of America—would never be the same again.

(Top) Through the years Davison County has had relatively few labor problems, but there were occasions—particularly in the railroad and meat-packing industries—when friction occurred. These Omaha line workers made their union solidarity perfectly clear. William Timmins collection.

Lawrence and Herman Bauer were members of the Ethan baseball team which played in the old Corn Belt League. A new ball park was built in 1930 and drew large crowds during the depression years. Dimock was Ethan's arch-rival. Dorothy Feiner collection.

Switch engines and main-line locomotives of the C.M.&St.P. were a common sight during the heyday of railroading in Mitchell as were the several hundred employees in the familiar overalls whose pay-checks were vital to the city's economy. Dr. Richard I. Porter collection.

The Turner Produce Company on Railroad Street was succeeded by the Armour Creamery which was a major employer in Mitchell during and after the Dirty Thirties. Chicken-pluckers, egg-crackers, butter-wrappers, churn boys and drivers of the familiar yellow Armour's trucks unionized after World War II and the plant closed in 1968. Mitchell Area Historical Society.

FOX DE LUXE
HOTEL

CHAPTER 9
The Aftermath of War: A New Era

In many ways 1945 became a line of demarcation separating two historical eras, and Davison County shared the change with the rest of the country. The scope of the war just ended; the extensive technological developments it fostered; the threat of nuclear destruction in any future military involvement; ever-widening chinks in age-old economic, social, political and religious foundations—all began to affect traditional American living patterns.

A far more mobile society grew out of a seemingly universal obsession of returning service people to own a new automobile as a symbol of self-freedom. Young veterans who had been exposed to the far reaches of the globe could not all be held in their native South Dakota, but those who left were replaced by out-of-staters who had appreciated the "elbow room" and lifestyle they had observed during service assignments in Mitchell, Sioux Falls, Provo and elsewhere—or who had met and married South Dakota girls during their military hitches.

Dakota Wesleyan and other state colleges benefited from the G.I. Bill. Good crops and favorable prices made it possible for farmers to pay off past indebtedness; and the Rural Electrification Administration—created in 1935 as a New Deal program—speeded up the wiring of rural residences in time for the television age. The elimination of government controls made gasoline, automobiles and shotgun shells available for a revived invasion of tourists and pheasant hunters, and the Corn Palace became a national attraction for camera-carrying travelers year around.

However, the general upbeat atmosphere of the post-war years was marred by more fires. Ethan lost its three grain elevators in a wind-swept blaze on April 22, 1946. Several months earlier, on December 16, 1945, the original Abbott House—founded in 1939 for homeless children and named for Grace Abbott, nationally known child welfare worker—was destroyed. Fortunately no lives were lost as director Robert Hahn, his family and thirteen young girls escaped in their night clothes in weather ten degrees below zero. The children were moved to the former home of Stephen F. Scallin, Sr., long-time Mitchell druggist, until a permanent facility could be provided. Further tragedy struck in 1946 when John Lindsey, the superintendent of the Mitchell public schools for more than a

(Opposite page and following page) On April 14, 1950, the four-story Widmann Hotel burned in a blaze which threatened much of Mitchell's Main Street. The fire drew almost as many spectators as a Corn Palace Week midway. Fortunately, all occupants escaped without loss of life. Mitchell Area Historical Society/Rodney and Dorothy Prather photos.

quarter century, was killed, along with his wife and two young teachers, in a three-car accident west of Mount Vernon.

On a brighter note, Lawrence Welk broke all attendance records at the Corn Palace in 1948 as 44,593 fans paid an average of $1.50 per ticket to see the Champagne Music Man. Many had followed his career closely and had danced to his earlier Hotsy Totsy Boys and Honolulu Fruit Gum Orchestra. (The record stood until 1966 when Tennessee Ernie Ford and the Singing Young Americans drew standing-room-only crowds totaling 52,892, the greatest number in the first hundred years of the Corn Palace history.)

The Corn Palace, incidentally, provided the studio for Davison County's first radio station when KGDA began broadcasting on April 6, 1930. Its transmitter was located on Radio Point extending out into Lake Mitchell, and auto dealer Jack Verschoor was president of the group of businessmen who backed the venture. Like its contemporaries in Yankton and Sioux Falls, KGDA featured mostly live programming in that still embryonic age of commercial radio. O. W. Coursey—local historian, writer and Spanish-American War veteran—made periodic speeches, while Hip Haynes and his orchestra provided musical interludes. Unfortunately, the station did not survive, although one of its announcers, Johnny Olson, worked his way up the ladder of success to national network prominence on "The Price Is Right" and other programs.

Following World War II, a new station—Radio KMHK—went on the air on July 11, 1947, from its studios in the Mitchell National Bank Building. Raymond V. Eppel, its founder, played organ music on the air in the early days; Davison County listeners heard Amos and Andy, Jack Benny, Fibber Magee and Molly and The Shadow on their own local station which was affiliated with the Mutual Broadcasting Company. In 1949 Eppel, who served on the Corn Palace committee for 22 years, acquired the unique but appropriate KORN call letters originally assigned to Fremont, Nebraska. The Mitchell Broadcasting Association—which he headed—also added Television Channel 5 in June of 1960. Eppel died in 1977 at age 69. Two years earlier the radio station he had pioneered was sold to Korn Palace Broadcasting, Inc., consisting of co-owners Dean L. DeSchepper, Arthur C. Rew, Marlyn Christensen, Robert W. Anton and Michael E. Opiola. KORN-TV was sold to Buford Television, Inc., and the call letters changed to KXON-TV.

In 1950 the county population reversed the depression and wartime downward trend when the U.S. Census reported 16,522 residents. However, Mitchell accounted for 12,123 of them, leaving a total of 4,399—or 26 percent—elsewhere in the county. Ten years earlier the non-Mitchell area had 30 percent of the population, and by 1970 this figure had dropped to 22 percent. The movement from farms and small towns to the larger cities was duplicated throughout South Dakota and was to have a notable effect on the rural economy.

Moving the Betts Grain Company's elevator was a major balancing feat. The small town of Betts —located on the rail line between Mitchell and Mount Vernon and named for State Senator A. H. Betts—flourished for almost half a century before a tornado and the Great Depression contributed to its demise. Mitchell Area Historical Society.

The one-room country schools—there were once as many as 50 located throughout the county—were closed gradually and pupils were bussed into Mitchell, Ethan and Mount Vernon. Betts, the railroad village located halfway between Mitchell and Mount Vernon and named for elevator builder A. H. Betts, once had a general store, postoffice, a lumberyard, blacksmith shop and a few family residences. A tornado in 1925 started its decline, and it even-

Mitchell's first radio station, KGDA, had its transmitter on a spit of land extending into Lake Mitchell known as Radio Point. It began broadcasting on April 6, 1930, from a studio in the Corn Palace. Mitchell Area Historical Society.

tually disappeared. Loomis likewise fell victim to the changing times.

Fire—seemingly the continuing scourge of the county—struck again on April 14, 1950, when the four-story Widmann Hotel at First and Main was destroyed and adjacent buildings damaged in a blaze which the *Mitchell Gazette* called "the worst in the city's history." No lives were lost, however, as many of the hotel's 58 guests formed a human chain and were led through the smoke to safety; others were rescued through windows by firemen. Firefighters and equipment came from more than a dozen different towns—as far away as Yankton, Sioux Falls and Centerville—primarily because there was concern about Mitchell's entire Main Street.

Mayor Damon Clark urged all Mitchell restaurants to feed visiting firemen and the bill would be picked up by the city. The Red Cross also set up feeding stations, and American Legion members served coffee. Cots were made available in the armory for those who needed them. The hotel—then under out-of-state ownership—had been built in the early 1900s by Fred Widmann, a German immigrant who came to Davison County in 1882 and established a successful liquor business, dance hall and bowling alley.

Of global concern, meanwhile, the specter of communism added a bit of edginess to an otherwise peaceful period, and then on June 25, 1950, word was received that North Korean forces had launched an attack on the Republic of South Korea. Just eight days later U.S. troops went into action against the invaders, and all too soon the repercussions were felt in Davison County, despite the fact that war was never officially declared. It was a new experience for both the American public and those in uniform. The all-out effort of World War II was missing from the "police action," but for those who were drafted or recalled to active duty, it was certainly a real war.

As a pointed example, 1st Lt. John Stransky of Mitchell, a veteran of the previous conflict, was ordered back into the service and eventually was killed in action as a platoon leader with the 1st Cavalry Division. While he and other area men and women were called to the colors, it was mostly business as usual at home. Harry James and his band headlined the 1950 Corn Palace show; and Betty Grable, the trumpeter's wife and pinup girl of World War II, spent the week in Mitchell but was not part of the program.

There were some civil defense activities, of course. A hundred and seventy five volunteers took turns as around-the-clock air-spotters on the roof of the Mount Vernon school. A similar schedule was maintained in Mitchell atop the Baron Brothers Store. No enemy planes were ever sighted, and in time the war-that-wasn't-a-war came to its debated conclusion.

At that point in history, it had been virtually forgotten by most residents that Davison County's towns and farmsteads were really by-products of railroad development. For seven decades the criss-crossing tracks were the lifeblood arteries of the region as both passenger and freight trains were taken for granted. Following World War II, though, an accelerated transportation evolution was taking place. Diesel engines replaced the old steam locomotives—but more significantly, semi-trucks and private automobiles became the preferred choices for commerce and personal travel. The paving of Highways 16 and 37—although not as historically romantic as the coming of the railroad—nonetheless had an equally vital impact.

In 1970 Tennessee Ernie Ford and the Singing Young Americans returned to the Corn Palace for a repeat performance. Four years earlier they topped Lawrence Welk's 1948 attendance record when they played to standing-room-only crowds totaling 52,892, the greatest number in the first hundred years of the exposition's history. Mitchell Area Historical Society.

No longer did the daily passenger trains bring the mail, the out-of-town newspapers and the traveling salesmen. Motels succeeded the downtown hotels. Cattle cars and track-side stockyards became obsolete, and once bustling depots gradually went the way of the livery stables.

On September 30, 1951, the Milwaukee Road's train No. 2 was the last regularly scheduled passenger train to serve Mitchell. There was no fanfare connected to the historic milestone; it went virtually unnoticed except by those intimately involved, like brakeman Cal Wieland. After that there were some combination trains and connecting runs with the transcontinental line at Aberdeen, but for all intents and purposes, the end of an era had come.

Freight trains continued to run, but railroad revenues plummeted until the Milwaukee Road finally filed for bankruptcy in 1978. According to the *Daily Republic*, the Chicago and North Western petitioned to close its Mitchell station that same year. Despite protests from shippers, the last train on the old Omaha line chugged into town on November 14, 1980, and left the next day, hauling a load of company property back to Sioux Falls.

Most seriously affected by the Milwaukee's action, of course, were Mount Vernon and Ethan, Loomis and Betts having already ceased to exist as recognizable towns. Mitchell, with its dominant population and strategic location on Interstate 90—which replaced the narrow, two-lane Highway 16 across the state—made the necessary transition and, except for occasional minor setbacks, continued to prosper. Meanwhile, the two smaller towns settled into quiet existence with limited business services but with a way of life preferred by long-time residents, retired farm folks and some younger people teaching in the schools and otherwise escaping the drawbacks of bigger cities.

The recent history of the county is still being shaped, of course. Businesses come and go. The population is more transient. Problems and challenges of schools, utilities and environmental concerns continue with solutions not yet finalized. Later developments need time to simmer and mature for future chroniclers to record. There is obviously much more to come; and, to borrow from William Shakespeare: What's past is merely prologue!

The crowded side tracks indicated Mitchell's once great importance as a railroad center. Then, in later years, the Milwaukee Road declared bankruptcy and the Chicago and North Western abandoned the old Omaha line. Eventually the state of South Dakota stepped in to prevent a total loss of service. Mitchell Area Historical Society.

Before the Milwaukee Road was dieselized after World War II, steam locomotives brought freight and passenger trains into Mitchell from all four directions. Memories of the roundhouse pond, the hobo jungle, traffic backed up at the Sanborn Street crossing before the overpass was built and old railroaders like Engineer Oscar J. "Zeke" Andres in the cab of No. 1084 became part of Davison County's nostalgic past. Dr. Richard I. Porter collection/Henry J. McCord photo.

S.D.H.S.A.A.
FOURTH ANNUAL
VERMILLION

CHAPTER 10

People, Politics, and Potpourri

Scores of prominent individuals have left their mark on Davison County through the years. Many, of course, were performers at the Corn Palace, but there were others as well. Suffragette Susan B. Anthony spoke in Mitchell in her crusade for women's rights, and saloon-smasher Carrie Nation came to lecture, too. Buffalo Bill Cody and his Wild West Show—including Annie Oakley and Sitting Bull—performed for an enthralled crowd in pre-Corn Palace days.

Presidents William J. McKinley, Theodore Roosevelt and Calvin Coolidge addressed assembled citizens on Main Street, as did presidential candidates William Howard Taft and William Jennings Bryan. When he was still U.S. Secretary of Commerce, Herbert Hoover appeared before a joint meeting of Mitchell service clubs.

James Earle Fraser, the renowned sculptor who designed the buffalo nickel, came to the county with his father, a railroad man, in the early 1880s. They lived in a boxcar for a time and later on a ranch where the budding artist was said to have carved Western figures from local chalkstone. His companionship with Indian youngsters also supposedly influenced his later work, which included his masterpiece, "The End of the Trail," the statue of the weary Indian on his equally weary pony.

Oscar Howe, the Yanktonai Sioux who was born on the Crow Creek Reservation in 1915, was a late graduate of Dakota Wesleyan in 1952 following overseas army service during World War II. For more than 20 years he designed the Corn Palace decorations. Before his death in 1983, his stylized mystic Indian art had become widely acclaimed and extremely valuable, a far cry from the 50 cents he received for the first painting he sold. He served on the art faculty at his alma mater and the University of South Dakota and was recognized as the state's artist laureate.

Similarly noted as South Dakota's first poet laureate, Charles Badger Clark, Jr., called himself a P.K.—"preacher's kid"—and originally came to Mitchell as a shy first-grader, attending the old wooden Whittier School. Later in life he credited a teacher—Miss Fanny Foster—with inspiring him with the confidence he previously lacked. After further elementary education in Huron and high school in Deadwood, he returned to Mitchell in 1902 to enroll at Dakota Wesleyan. In his own words, he had a very "undistinguished career"

(Opposite page) Despite numerous football and basketball titles, Mitchell High School won its only state track championship in nine decades in 1908. Photographer Martin K. Eliason failed to identify the runners in the classic photo above. Bill Timmins collection.

In World War II George McGovern flew 35 combat missions over Europe as pilot of a B-24 bomber, the "Dakota Queen." He was awarded the Distinguished Flying Cross at age 22. Author's collection.

lasting just one year. It was rumored that he was expelled for putting a goat in a dormitory. After that, he joined a colonizing expedition to Cuba headed by E. D. Kerr of Mitchell. In 1923 D.W.U. recognized his literary talents by awarding him an honorary Doctor of Letters degree.

While his son received the greater notoriety, Reverend C. B. Clark, Sr., made a much more significant contribution to the history of Davison County. As a young circuit-riding Methodist minister in Iowa, he had overworked himself to a state of ill health. To recover, he moved his family to a homestead in Aurora County, D. T., where he regained his strength but disliked the demands of farming. Accepting a pastorate in Mitchell, he returned to his calling and eventually became superintendent of the Mitchell district of his denomination and one of the principal founders of Dakota Wesleyan. He received an honorary doctorate from the school long before his son did, and after his death in 1921 at age 82, he was buried in Mitchell's Graceland Cemetery where both his wives are also interred.

Another son of a Methodist minister—George Stanley McGovern, born at Avon on July 19, 1922—undoubtedly brought more notoriety to Davison County than any other person when he became the Democratic nominee for president in 1972. McGovern was a graduate of both Mitchell High School and Dakota Wesleyan where he excelled in debate and twice won the South Dakota Peace Oratory contest. He played piano for Sunday School, and his first career plan was to follow in his father's footsteps; but after serving as a student minister at Diamond Lake, Illinois, and attending Garrett Theological Seminary in Evanston, he came to the conclusion that his calling lay in the academic field and he switched to nearby Northwestern University to earn his doctorate in history.

On October 31, 1943—on a three-day pass from flight training at Muskogee, Oklahoma—he married Eleanor Stegeberg of

Woonsocket against whom he had debated in high school and who had attended Dakota Wesleyan one year before becoming a secretary for two prominent Democratic attorneys in Mitchell, former U.S. Senator Herbert Hitchcock and Fred Nichol, later a federal judge. The ceremony was performed by George's father, Reverend Joseph McGovern, ex-coal miner and minor league baseball player turned preacher.

After completing his work at Northwestern, the younger McGovern returned to his alma mater as a $4,500-a-year professor of history. In the meantime, four of their five children had been born as he and Eleanor struggled to subsist on his G.I. Bill money and meager teaching fellowships. He enjoyed teaching, but by this time politics was in his blood and he made the difficult decision to leave Dakota Wesleyan to become executive secretary of the state's Democratic Party, then with almost no effective organization.

Although he became an anti-war advocate because of his opposition to the U.S. involvement in Vietnam, he had distinguished himself in World War II as pilot of a B-24 Liberator bomber aptly titled the "Dakota Queen." He flew 35 combat missions in Europe and was awarded the Distinguished Flying Cross at age 22. Finally, in 1956—after energizing the state's lethargic Democrats—he began his up-by-the-bootstraps political climb. Against what some considered insurmountable odds, he defeated a confident incumbent, Harold O. Lovre, for a seat in the U.S. House of Representatives. He won a re-election bid against ex-Governor Joe Foss, but failed in a run against Senator Karl Mundt in 1960.

President John F. Kennedy then appointed the 38-year-old McGovern (who once candled eggs for 40 cents an hour) as head of the new Food for Peace program, a position which thrust him into greater national prominence. In 1962 he returned to South Dakota to challenge Senator Francis H. Case, coincidentally, like McGovern, son of a Methodist minister and a 1918 graduate of D.W.U. in history. However, Case died of a heart attack that spring, and Lieutenant Governor Joseph H. Bottum was chosen to fill out his term and then become the Re-

A graduate of Mitchell High School and Dakota Wesleyan, George McGovern was the Democratic candidate for the U. S. presidency in 1972, losing to Richard M. Nixon. As a United States senator from his native state and director of President John F. Kennedy's Food for Peace program, he gained international prominence. Dakota Wesleyan University.

publican candidate opposing the former professor and congressman. After a bitter campaign, McGovern emerged the apparent winner by a mere 100 votes out of more than a quarter of a million ballots cast. A recount finally assured him of victory by a margin of just 597. He served in the Senate until his unsuccessful bid to replace President Richard M. Nixon. When he established his residence elsewhere, he sold his Mitchell home to the First Lutheran Church which used it as a parsonage until its eventual demolition.

Joe Robbie, who became nationally known as owner of the Miami Dolphins professional football team, was—at least for a time—considered an "adopted son" of Davison County. A Navy veteran and Bronze Star winner for action in the South Pacific, the Sisseton native began his law practice in Mitchell. Like McGovern, he was a collegiate debate champion and taught at Dakota Wesleyan. After serving a term in the South Dakota House of Representatives, he was named state chairman of the Democratic Party and in 1950 he failed in an attempt to unseat popular Governor Sigurd Anderson. After that he moved to Minneapolis as regional director of the Office of Price Stabilization and eventually acquired the football expansion franchise in the Florida city. He left a legacy in Mitchell in the form of athletic fields at D.W.U., designated as the Joseph and Jennie Robbie Sports Complex.

Throughout its history Davison County has had its share of able leaders: teachers, ministers, mayors, commissioners, legislators, law officers, librarians, entrepreneurs and others not cited elsewhere in this narrative. Dedicated women have played important—but often unsung—roles in various areas of community service, especially in education, the arts, charitable works and health care.

Mabel O. Woods, the administrator of the Methodist Hospital from 1923 to 1947, deserves special mention for guiding the institution through the Great Depression and World War II. In 1960 she was recipient of the city's highest honor, originally designated as the obviously sexist "Mr. Mitchell" award and first won by Monsignor John McHugh Brady, a former World War I chaplain and pastor of Holy Family Parish for 44 years until his death in 1963 at age 94. Another "Mr. Mitchell" honoree was Elsie Snow Hanson who "read the law" and became an attorney when it was still uncommon for women to enter that profession. Mrs. Clarence Hager, wife of the pastor of the first Methodist Episcopal Church in Mitchell, often took his place in the pulpit when he was ill or away, well before women were ordained. Years later, Florence K. Ronald became publisher of *The Daily Republic* following the death of her husband, Malcolm, and held that position until the publication was sold to Thomson Newspapers, Inc., a Canada-based international chain.

Almost a century after the school's founding, the Dakota Wesleyan cheerleaders of 1980-81 embellished the campus sign with their presence. Students adopted Blue and White as the school colors in 1902. Dakota Wesleyan University.

It was a long time in coming, but in 1924 Celia M. Kelley, a Republican and former teacher, was elected to the South Dakota House of Representatives, the first Davison County woman to serve in the state legislature. Her son William preceded her in Pierre, and her husband followed them both in 1929. Democrat Mary E. Kotbra came to Dakota in 1880, graduated from Dakota Wesleyan—as did Celia Kelley—and after teaching school for five years, became actively involved in a poultry farm west of Mitchell. She served as president of the South Dakota Farm Women's Congress, and in 1926 was elected to the House at age 52, the only female member of that particular term.

Martha Carstens became one of the few lady sheriffs of a South Dakota county when she succeeded her husband George in the office in 1952. That was when sheriffs were limited to two consecutive two-year terms. The Carstens lived in an apartment adjacent to the jail, and Martha was George's lone deputy, cooking for the prisoners and handling administrative tasks. When she was elected, her husband became her deputy, and they operated pretty much as they had before until he was able to run—and be elected—again. Because of their residence, they were never free from the pressures of the work, and when George died unexpectedly of a heart attack in April of 1964, Martha completed his term, after which her 29-year-old deputy, Lyle Swenson, ran for the office and began an extended tenure of his own, including a term as president of the National Sheriff Association.

James Earle Fraser, who designed the buffalo nickel and gained lasting notoriety for sculpting his "End of the Train" masterpiece, lived in Davison County as a youth with his railroading father. It is said that he drew from his Dakota experiences to produce the works for which he became famous. South Dakota Magazine collection.

In Mitchell's long list of mayors dating back to Chauncey Burr, few have been more respected than Leonard B. "Bud" Williams. A native of the Corn Palace City, Williams served 26 years in the military service during and after World War II. He returned to his hometown, worked as director of the local YMCA and then as the coordinator of student activities at the Mitchell Vocational Technical Institute until his second retirement. He then entered city politics, was elected a councilman in 1985, and in the following year won a landslide victory in the campaign for mayor. In the first of his multiple terms, Mitchell was designated as "Community of the Year" by the late Governor George S. Mickelson. Williams credited the honor to what he called CPP: Collective Effort, Positive Thinking and Perserverance.

Davison County could boast other individuals of diverse interests and talents. Among them were Clinton P. Anderson, a D.W.U. graduate who served as U.S. Secretary of Agriculture under President Harry Truman, and Robert C. Kirkwood, manager of the F. W. Woolworth Company store in Mitchell during the 1930s who eventually became president of the giant retailing firm. Gary Altman—known on national television as Gary Owens—attended Dakota Wesleyan and began his broadcasting career on KGDA Radio. He later became widely recognized as the hand-on-the-ear announcer for the popular Dan Rowan-Dick Martin "Laugh-In" show.

There were others, of course, not all of whom can be recorded in this limited narrative. Ordell Braase, a three-sport star for the Kernels who led them to a state basketball championship and later an All-North Central Conference lineman for the University of South Dakota Coyotes, became an all-pro defensive end for the Baltimore Colts during the Johnny Unitas era. Another versatile Mitchell High School athlete was Richard L. "Dick" Green who made it to the major leagues as a second baseman for the Kansas City Athletics and played in the World Series with the Oakland A's in 1972, 1973 and 1974. His big league record included 1,288 games, 4,007 appearances at the plate and 80 homeruns.

Despite such outstanding stars as Braase and Green, though, when Davison County sports history is discussed, area old-timers invariably begin with one name: Arthur A. "Joe" Quintal. Born at Jefferson, South Dakota, on December 18, 1899, Quintal captained a championship Elk Point High School football team in 1917, and

—as a University of South Dakota Coyote—he ran 105 yards for a touchdown against the South Dakota State Jackrabbits in 1922, still considered a memorable feat in the state's sports annals. In 1926 he became athletic director and coach of all sports at Mitchell High School, winning six state basketball championships in the '30s and '40s and leading his young Kernels to enviable successes until he retired from active coaching in 1957. He remained with the school system as athletic director for eight more years and then went on to serve as a state senator from Davison and Sanborn counties from 1969 to 1975. He founded the Corn Palace Relays in 1947 and was named "Mr. Mitchell" in 1961. In 1984 the high school athletic field was named in his honor.

In a way, Joe Quintal was symbolic of the avid interest in sporting events of all kinds in Davison County going back to its earliest years. For instance, the 1882 Fourth of July celebration at the Mitchell Driving Park featured a baseball game ($25 to the winner), a 20-rod foot race ($10 for first place) and a half-mile free-for-all run (no prizes announced).

Before the turn of the century, baseball was played in township pastures as well as in the towns; and heated rivalries resulted. Dakota Wesleyan and Mitchell High School experimented with football as early as 1896 when teams from the cross-town institutions met in a scrimmage in front of College Hall on the D.W.U. campus (no score was recorded). Wesleyan played its first intercollegiate game against Yankton College on November 15, 1897, losing 40-12. The following year the Tumbleweeds (as the team was often called) won the mythical state championship. Years later, in 1919,

the Blue and White got belated sweet revenge for Yankton College's inaugural win. The seemingly invincible Greyhounds had outscored their opponents 409-0 before the final Thanksgiving Day game on a frozen field in the Mother City with the temperature hovering around zero. When the fiercely fought contest ended in darkness 12 1/2 minutes short of regulation time, Dakota Wesleyan had won 20-6. Needless to say, after that the rivalry between the "Methodists" and the "Congregationalists" (as the sportswriters of the day labeled them) remained intense long after the historic upset was forgotten by almost everyone except sports historians.

The Mount Vernon Mustangs won nine district basketball titles in ten years from 1939 to 1948, while the Ethan Rustlers nine-man football team made it to the first playoffs in the Dakota Dome at Vermillion, losing to Bridgewater for a still enviable 9-1 season. When the Ethan girls basketball team qualified for the state tournament that same year, one of their cheerleaders—Mary Belitz—provided an inspirational sidelight because she had been blind since birth. Twice the Notre Dame Comets of Mitchell won the South Dakota State Catholic Basketball Tournament, in 1954 and 1959.

It goes without saying that in the format and size of this volume, not even all of the major highlights of the athletic history of Davison County can be chronicled: the many trophies won in various sports, the fast-pitch and later-day slow-pitch softball tournaments, the belated entry of women into competitive athletics, American Legion and Basin League baseball, golf, track, wrestling, tennis, volleyball, gymnastics, bowling, the growing interest in soccer and even horseshoe-pitching.

"Mandy's Minstrels" was a 1928 production of the Eastern Star Lodge of Mitchell. In an era when Al Jolson was introducing black-face musicals, little thought was given to possible racial insensitivity and no demeaning harm was intended. In 1921 Freeman Gosden and Charles Correll, who later became the Amos and Andy of radio fame, were in Mitchell as directors of a minstrel show sponsored by the American Legion. Mitchell Area Historical Society.

Widely recognized names like Leo Harmon, known as one of the state's finest athletic officials; D.W.U.'s Coach Lester C. Belding, an All-American end from Iowa; Mark Payne, who set a world's record with a 63-yard dropkick to defeat Northern Normal in 1915; Gary Munsen who coached the Kernels to both boys' and girls' high school basketball championships; Greg Farrar of Dakota Wesleyan who threw a basketball 71 feet through the hoop with one second left on the clock to beat Huron College for the South Dakota Intercollegiate Conference title in 1974; Scott Morgan, the "all-everything" basketball ace of the Kernels and the D.W.U. Tigers; and even Ben Obrembt, elevator operator and playing manager of the Ethan baseball team in the 1950s who was forever kidded about being slow of foot after he hit a ball to the centerfield fence and was thrown out going into first base—all of them, sorry to say, must be relegated to mere mention in a story which spans more than a century.

As a young man Leonard B. "Bud" Williams (at left) worked as a laborer for Rozum Motors, served 26 years in the U. S. military and returned to his hometown to win repeated terms as Mitchell's mayor. William's father came to the Corn Palace City as supervisor of the Milwaukee Road's coal-loading operation. He was killed in a railroading accident in 1946. Rozum Motors.

The history of the county is garnished with its share of legend and lore, fiction, fabrication, warped facts and, of course, some interesting true incidents to add a little spice to the overall tale. Here are a few samples in this potpourri chapter, with the reader responsible for deciding into which category they fit. There was, for instance, the unnamed midwife of Ethan who claimed to have invented a pill to cure everything. It was rumored that she was beaten to death by another woman from Dimock who sold get-well cards.

Also at Ethan, old-timers told of Pete Breck, Sr., who had a still for making moonshine during the prohibition era. He supposedly sold wine and home brew for 25 cents a quart, and some men brought their own jugs when they stopped by his house after church on Sundays. They said he kept his supplies in a hole under his barn.

In 1892, during one of the state's periodic dry spells, a representative of the Interstate Artificial Rain Company met with farmers from Davison and other counties and promised to make it rain for $500. If it did, he would then sell his secret to them for $2,500. It didn't!

A railroad error was apparently responsible for the location of the Fullerton Lumber Company in Mitchell. Three brothers—Thomas, George and James Fullerton—intended to start their firm in Sioux City, Iowa, but the carload of lumber they had purchased in 1881 was mis-sent to Mitchell. When they began to make sales right from the car, they decided to remain in the new Davison County town from which the extensive Fullerton chain eventually expanded throughout the Upper Midwest.

The Corn Palace festival has been fortunate in its lack of tragic events during its century-long existence. One of the saddest mishaps, however, occurred in 1950 when Kurt Kienast—a 38-year-old aerialist from Chicago billed as the Great Kurt—fell to his death as hundreds of spectators, including his wife and 2 1/2-year-old daughter, watched the free show.

In 1884 the *Mitchell Capital* reported that an "expert" found gold in paying quantities near the town. The metal supposedly was assayed in Chicago and was said to be of high quality, so the unnamed expert was negotiating for the land on which the ore was located. The paper predicted a possible "gold craze," but nothing came of it. Local citizens seemed to be happier about the new street sprinkler which was keeping down the dust on Main Street.

Jerry Phelps was Ethan's veterinarian for half a century. He was also a champion checker player and took his checkerboard with him wherever he went. He always carried a lantern on his buggy for night calls, and when he got a Chevrolet coupe, he hung the lantern on the spare tire.

O. E. Browne, who came to Davison County in 1883 and was the principal of Mount Vernon's old wooden school house for 12 years, was an early-day conservationist. In 1902 he divided a fireguard strip around the school grounds into small plots and let his students file a "claim" on each. They then had to plant a tree on their lots, giving each tree a name. Unfortunately, neither the school (which burned in 1917) nor the 174 trees—with such names as "Noah", "Ham," "Shem," "Jeffeth" and "Sir Francis Drake"—survived.

Mitchell was the product of the railroad. This aerial photo, looking from west to east, showed the Milwaukee Road complex on the south edge of the city, with roundhouse, coal tower and roundhouse pond. Mitchell Area Historical Society.

Tourists of the early 1920s traveling to and from the Black Hills on graveled roads pitched their tents in Mitchell's Hitchcock Park in the era before motels and Interstate 90. Mitchell Area Historical Society.

In 1891 Dr. John Tatum was fined $20 and costs for using indecent language on the street in Mount Vernon. He was arrested as the result of a horse-whipping episode. Two years earlier, according to the *Daily Republican,* Ed Duane of Mitchell escaped the law when Mrs. George Rowley's horse jumped in front of his gig, upsetting it, badly bruising Ed and making him angry beyond expression. The paper added that some observers said he was angry *with* expression because of "the decidedly blue tint he gave the air."

According to local historian Leon W. Jenks, the late Lawrence Welk left a debt in Ethan. After Welk and his three-piece band had played for a dance in Fred Weepie's Hall in the late 1920s, the accordionist couldn't get his car to start. Weepie put in a new battery, and because Welk didn't have enough money, he said he'd pay the bill the next time he came to Ethan. He never played in Ethan again, and the battery was never paid for.

Speaking of celebrities, Corn Palace committee members recalled that Jack Benny insisted on a bodyguard when he walked out on the street—but hardly anybody paid any attention to him. Paul Whiteman apparently tippled too much so that it was obvious during the national broadcast of the Chesterfield Hour from the Palace, and it was said that he lost the lucrative cigarette-sponsored program because of it. Andy Williams supposedly demanded the most special treatment, but Red Skelton came to the festival several days ahead of his scheduled performance and had a grand time mingling with the Main Street crowd—without bodyguard.

In 1915 two wanted men arrived in Ethan on a freight train, threatened patrons in a saloon with a meat cleaver and were a general menace on the street. Dan Sullivan, the town's first butcher and later a cattle buyer, gave chase and shot one of them dead. The other escaped. The victim of Sullivan's true aim, local lore has it, was put in a gunny sack and shipped to Vermillion for experiments in the laboratory there.

Another Corn Palace memory occurred in 1933 when the committee—in trying to keep up with the times—booked a fan dancer to take advantage of the publicity Sally Rand had generated at Chicago's Century of Progress exposition. There was vigorous local opposition to such a risque act, but the dance went on before a packed house. The audience watched the performance in absolute silence, and there was no applause when it ended. However, despite the depression, the committee was able to meet all its obligations and even to refund the pledges made to underwrite possible losses—but the fan dancer was never invited back.

Old files of the *Mitchell Capital*, the *Daily Republic(an)*, the *Mount Vernon News*, the *Ethan Enterprise* (later combined with the *Mitchell Gazette* to become the *Davison County Tribune*)—even the German language *Dakota Post* (1897-1902) and *Sud-Dakota Nachrichten* (1890-1899)—have an ample share of reports of murders and mayhem, bootleggers and ladies of the night, fines for using a stud horse behind the livery stable, political chicanery, and—as the auction ads say—much more "too numerous to mention." The froth, along with the solid news of the day, make up the history of any community. Davison County is no exception.

The 1917 Dakota Wesleyan football team, boasting "a wonderful mastery of the forward pass," opened the season with a 91-0 victory over Augustana College of Canton. The remainder of the schedule included three losses, two wins and two ties. The team included future U. S. Senator Francis Case, a 145-pound end who suffered a broken clavicle. Dakota Wesleyan University/Harry B. Hersey photo.

MBC
MBC
MBC
MBC
MBC
MBC
MBC
MBC
MBC
MBC
1931

Even though Mitchell High School coach Joe Quintal called basketball "a sissy game," the sport shared with baseball great popularity throughout the county. All schools had teams, including the Mitchell Business College, left (Bertha Ness collection). The Mount Vernon independent team, right (Mount Vernon Library), went undefeated in 1920-21.

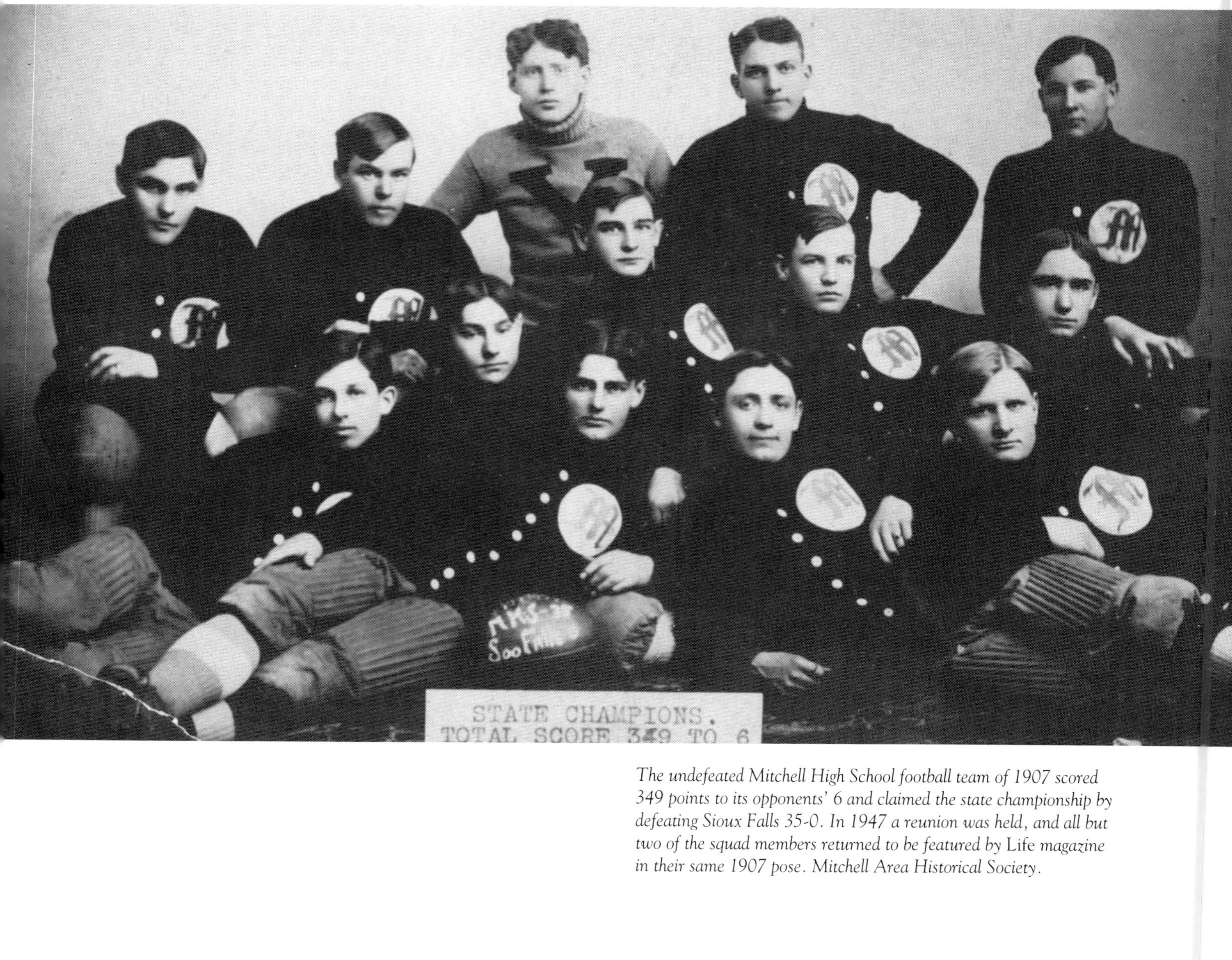

The undefeated Mitchell High School football team of 1907 scored 349 points to its opponents' 6 and claimed the state championship by defeating Sioux Falls 35-0. In 1947 a reunion was held, and all but two of the squad members returned to be featured by Life *magazine in their same 1907 pose. Mitchell Area Historical Society.*

Among the many championships won by Mitchell athletes was the 1951 state American Legion baseball title. Rozum Motors sponsored the winning team. Rozum Motors collection.

In 1941 Notre Dame High School fielded its first six-man football team. Unfortunately, game uniforms didn't arrive in time for the opening game against Spencer, but the Comets played anyhow. Coach Maurice "Moe" Shevlin (back row, center) became well known in South Dakota athletic circles. Mitchell Area Historical Society.

Gary C. Munsen ranks as one of the winningest coaches in South Dakota high school basketball history. In 20 years his Mitchell Kernel boys won five state championships and eight Eastern South Dakota Conference titles, five of them in a row. The 1984-85 team was undefeated in 23 games. In four years as coach of the M.H.S. girls, his Lady Kernels have been state champs twice, and the 1992 five duplicated the boys' 23-0 record. The Daily Republic/*Korrie Wenzel photo.*

This vintage aerial photo of Mitchell in the 1930s included the remains of the Milwaukee roundhouse (lower left), so familiar to old-timers, as well as the roundhouse pond, an early-day recreational area for youngsters and camp site for hoboes. Dr. Richard I. Porter collection.

The 14,000 square foot Soukup & Thomas International Balloon & Airship Museum brought a new dimension to Mitchell's tourism attractions. As a result, multi-colored hot air and helium balloons were to become familiar and exciting sights over the Davison County prairie. Pat Helgeland photo.

EPILOGUE

Toward a New Century

History is made every minute of every day but written history requires time to simmer: for on-going events to reach fruition; for the lives of living individuals, existing business firms, various organizations, schools, churches and government entities to work out their destinies—for good or bad—before the final record can be preserved for posterity.

Chroniclers of history should never write in the present tense because the common expression "here today, gone tomorrow" can quickly invalidate a situation which, at the moment, seems so secure, so unchanging. Davison County, like all counties everywhere, has experienced that reality.

Ever since the first settlement at Firesteel, the county and its three surviving towns have had to make adjustments to the vagaries of the times: natural disasters, fires, economic ups-and-downs, demographic shifting and the evolution of technology and transportation choices. Over the years merchants, manufacturers, morticians, milliners and money-lenders have set up shop, prospered, then faded away for one reason or another to be replaced by still other optimistic grocers, restaurateurs, lawyers, doctors, butchers, bakers, saloon keepers and auto dealers.

Packing plants like Erion's, Armour's and George A. Hormel & Company thrived, then disappeared. Motels replaced the hotels which had been so important in the days of railroad travel. Hotels seemed particularly susceptible to fires which destroyed the Alexander Mitchell (1913), the Widmann (1950), the Landmark (1977) and finally the Lawler (1992). The latter—built in the 1920s and bearing an historical Mitchell name—was originally a one-story factory before a second floor was added and it was converted into a lodging facility. Located just a block from the Corn

The Enchanted World Doll Museum in Mitchell was opened to the public in 1982, displaying a collection of more than 4,000 dolls begun by the late Sheldon F. Reese in 1937 when his sister asked him to buy ethnic dolls for her during his world travels. Eunice Reese was named lifetime curator of the unrivaled exhibit. Clyde Goin photo.

(Top) Lake Mitchell did not exist 10 centuries ago when a band of hunter-farmers lived in some 70 dirt-floor lodges in their fortified enclave on the above site. Now recognized as a National Archaelogical Landmark, the Mitchell Prehistoric Indian Village was first mapped in 1922 and later excavated, but the true identity of the residents remains shrouded in mystery. Pat Helgeland photo.

(Bottom) The first Randall grocery store came to Mitchell in 1952, and the Corn Palace City later became the headquarters for the company's multi-state operation. Participating in a ceremonial ground-breaking in 1992 for a new store were, left to right: Ron Randall, president of the firm; Mayor L. B. "Bud" Williams; Bill Bell, Randall's director of operations; and Bryan Hisel, executive director of the Mitchell Chamber of Commerce. Debra Kucera photo.

Palace, it was especially convenient for performers who could walk to their waiting audiences.

There were other fires, too, at Prairie Market, the Super City Shopping Center and the Village Bowl. Nature also took its toll as a tornado struck the west side of Mitchell on May 21, 1962, and during the ensuing year many of the county's majestic old trees fell victim to Dutch Elm disease.

The Contentious Sixties brought spasms of unrest to normally conservative Dakota Wesleyan. Popular Jack Early, then the university's president who could call most students by name as he walked across the campus, was hanged in effigy from *The Daily Republic* building's sign following a flare-up over interracial dating. KKK initials were painted on Smith Hall, and there was an explosion in one of the dormitories. The Vietnam War spawned further protest, but in time traditional values prevailed.

There were numerous business adjustments in Mitchell. Gordon F. Thomsen's Trail King Industries and Toshiba America Information Systems, Inc., became major employers. In 1952 F. Dwain "Doc" Randall and his partner, Burdell Spies, extended their grocery operation to Mitchell. Randall—who had begun his career as a stock boy for Council Oak Foods in Sioux City, Iowa—later divided his interests with Spies and established Randall Foods, Inc., opening stores in more than three dozen cities in seven states before his death in 1981 at age 69. He maintained his corporate headquarters in Mitchell.

Ross Laboratories which manufactured Similac, a powdered baby formula, was succeeded by a branch plant of the 3M Company which produced copy machine supplies. Herter's, a maker of outdoor sporting equipment, had a short-lived existence in Mitchell after which its plant was taken over by the Syncom Division of Schwann's Sales Enterprises, not to make ice cream, but computer accessories. The Educator Supply Company, founded in 1894 by Harry L. Bras and known throughout the state for its school supplies and books, was purchased by McLeod's Printing Company in 1979, McLeod's itself tracing its lineage to the Mitchell Printing Company which dated back to 1885.

In a move lauded by health-planners, St. Joseph's and the Methodist Hospitals joined forces with expanded but non-duplicated facilities under a new name, Queen of Peace. The Soukup & Thomas International Balloon & Airship Museum moved to Mitchell from Tyndall and located within a block of the Corn Palace. Along with the Enchanted World Doll Museum just across the street, the city had three major tourist attractions virtually adjacent to one another.

These, of course, were just some of the examples of the changing enterprises in Mitchell. Unfortunately, in the smaller towns permanent closure was the most common occurrence as a more mobile, auto-dominated citizenry traveled to larger cities for the shopping which was once done mostly at home.

Schools likewise expanded, multiplied or disappeared as the result of shifting populations. Mount Vernon benefited when a new high school was built; Ethan struggled to maintain enrollment. The Mitchell Business College, founded in 1926, came and went. So, too, did Notre Dame Junior College which merged with Presentation Junior College of Aberdeen in 1951 after graduating 1,376 students in its 29 years of existence. Twenty years later Notre Dame High School also closed. To offset the losses, Mitchell Vocational Technical Institute was founded in 1968 to provide post-high school training in a variety of programs in trades and services.

As both the social and economic hub of the county, Mitchell began its look to the future with a program called Vision 2000, a project headed by another in the lengthening line of Dakota Wesleyan presidents, Jim Beddow. With a new century on the horizon, there was a need to kindle an economic rejuvenation and to overcome what the *Argus Leader* of Sioux Falls termed "a demographic stall."

No doubt Davison County will have its ups and downs in the 21st century just as it had in pioneer days and the years in between; but, God willing, the Jim River will continue to flow and the Corn Palace will go on attracting new generations with sophisticated video cameras instead of the Kodak Brownies of yesterday. However, as important as the future may be, the focus of this book is on the past and the memories it generates: of basketball games in Weepie's Hall, bowery dances at Dreamland, skating on the roundhouse pond, of hoboes and gypsies, daily passenger trains, the dust and grasshoppers of the 1930s, Sunday baseball, ten-cent movies, Fourth of July parades, horse-drawn plows and tractors with lugs, the crackling static of early-day radios, country schools with outdoor biffies, picnics at Hitchcock Park, frozen long johns on the wash line, etc., etc., etc. Happy nostalgia!

(Top) Trail King Industries, founded by Gordon F. Thomsen, became one of Davison County's largest employers. The company produced what was reputedly the world's largest trailer with 126 wheels and a 300-ton capacity, a challenging departure from its numerous models marketed throughout the U. S. and beyond. Trail King Industries, Inc., photo.

(Bottom) Arthur A. "Joe" Quintal became a Davison County sports legend as coach of the Mitchell High School Kernels. After his retirement he was honored as "Mr. Mitchell" in 1961, and the high school athletic field was named for him in 1984. Bob Brooks collection.

Among the many attractions at the Corn Palace exposition through the years were the Budweiser Clydesdale horses. Mitchell Area Historical Society/Clyde Goin photo.

Railroad tracks fading into the sunset symbolized the end of an era for Davison County. The Omaha line was abandoned, and the State of South Dakota eventually took over the bankrupt Milwaukee's tracks to retain essential freight service—but the glory days of rail transportation became an historic memory. Dr. Richard I. Porter photo.

"Cornelius" became an appropriate mascot for the Mitchell High School athletic teams, the Kernels. The corn theme has been a Mitchell tradition since 1892. Deb Kuchera photo.

The annual stripping of the previous year's decorations and putting a new face on the Corn Palace has always been a tedious and challenging process. Earlier geometric patterns were succeeded by theme designs, often reflecting events of the contemporary period. Clyde Goin photo.

BIBLIOGRAPHY

The material for this book has come from a wide variety of sources, including the columns of *The Daily Republic* of Mitchell and its journalistic predecessors, *The Mitchell Gazette, The Ethan Enterprise, The Mount Vernon News* and other newspapers; the memoirs of pioneers like Louise Greene Hammer, Frederic E. Moses, Niles J. Dunham, Raymond J. Reitzel, Ethel Dowdell Abild and John R. White; miscellaneous clippings, student theses and scrapbooks; the collections of the Mitchell Area and South Dakota State Historical Societies; and from—among others—the publications listed below:

Abild, Ethel Dowdell. "Firesteel: Birthplace of Mitchell, South Dakota." *The Karl E. Mundt Historical & Educational Foundation Series No. 9, 13th Dakota History Conference.* Madison, S.D.: Dakota State College, 1982.

Bertsch, Garvin. *The Mitchell Rotary Club History, 1917-1988.* Mitchell, S.D.: privately published, 1988.

Boyce, W. D. *Industries of Mitchell, Dakota.* St. Paul, Minn.: The Pacific Publishing Co., 1884.

Brooks, Arthur F. *A Story of Mitchell (1880-1955).* Mitchell, S.D.: privately published, 1955.

Coursey, O. W. *A History of Dakota Wesleyan University for Fifty Years (1885-1935).* Mitchell, S.D.: Dakota Wesleyan University, 1954.

Cropp, Richard. "The Man Who Captured John Brown." *The Karl E. Mundt Historical & Educational Foundation Series No. 8, Selected Papers of the First Nine Dakota History Conferences, 1969-1977.* Madison, S.D.: Dakota State College, 1981.

Dunham, Niles J. *History of the Corn Palace.* Mitchell, S.D.: *The Mitchell Gazette,* 1912-13.

Graves, Berniece. *Ethan Centennial 1883.* Ethan, S.D.: Ethan Commercial Club, 1983.

Jenks, Leon W. *First 100 Years of Ethan.* Ethan, S.D.: privately printed, 1983.

Karolevitz, Robert F. *Challenge: The South Dakota Story.* Sioux Falls, S.D.: Brevet Press, Inc., 1975.

______. *With a Shirt Tail Full of Type: The Story of Newspapering in South Dakota.* Freeman, S.D.: South Dakota Press Association, 1982.

Lee, Robert. "The Burning of the Mitchell Mail: Justice or Injustice?" *South Dakota History,* Vol. 22, No. 3. Pierre, S.D.: South Dakota State Historical Society, 1992.

Mitchell Centennial History Committee. *Mitchell Re-Discovered.* Mitchell, S.D.: McLeod's Printing Co., 1980.

Schell, Herbert S. *A History of South Dakota.* Lincoln, Neb.: University of Nebraska Press, 1961.

Wilson, Dolores Barnes. *From the Wrong Side of the Tracks.* Stickney, S.D.: Argus Printers, 1980.

Wiseman, Maxine Schrader. *Dakota Dateline 1881-1956: The Story of Mount Vernon, South Dakota.* Mount Vernon, S.D.: *The Mount Vernon News,* 1956.

INDEX

Because Davison County appears throughout the book, it is not included in the index. South Dakota cities and towns are indicated by state unless they existed only in territorial days.

A

Abbott, Grace, 149
Abbott House, 149
Aberdeen, SD, 44, 84, 101, 154, 181
Abild, Ethel Dowdell, 184
Adams, C. W., 131
Adams, Harold L., 143
Agricultural Adjustment Act, 132
Alexander Mitchell Hotel, 29, 58, 179
Alexandria, SD, 25, 35
Allen, Arthur, 31
Allen, Ethan, 39
Alterton, Rufus F., 20, 27
Altman, Gary (Gary Owens), 163
Althen, Carl, 52
Althen, John, 52
Alton, IL, 22
Ambrose, Curtis, 20
American Legion Post No. 18, 144
Amert, Pat, 13
Amiotte, Arthur, 72
Amos and Andy, 151, 165
Anderson, Bill, 77
Anderson, Charlie, 113
Anderson, C. I., 63
Anderson, Clinton P., 163
Anderson, Joe, 113
Anderson, John, 113
Anderson, Gov. Sigurd, 160
Andres, Oscar J., 155
Anglum, Kate, 40
Anthony, Susan B., 157
Anton, Robert W., 151
Arland, Charles H., 35-37
Arlandton, DT (see Mount Vernon), 26, 36, 105
Arlington, SD, 36
Armour Creamery, 147
Armour's Packing Co., 179
Armstrong County, 18
Arneson's saloon, 26
Arnold, Eddy, 68
Atkinson, George, 113
Augustana College (Canton), 169
Aurora County, 35, 158
Avon, SD, 65, 158

B

Badger postoffice, 7
Badger Township, 35
Bailey, Ezra, 105
Bailey, James L., 144
Baker, Charley, 21
Baker School No. 4, 31
Baker Township, 23
Ball, Nellie, 31
Ball, Thomas, 31, 121
Ball, Dr. William R., 107
Baltimore Colts, 163
Baltimore, MD, 18
Barnes, A. H., 19
Baron Brothers Store, 153
Barton, Howard, 106
Bauer, George, 93
Bauer, Herman, 146
Bauer, Lawrence, 146
Beadle County, 31, 137
Beckwith, Louis E., 57, 136
Beddow, Jim, 181
Belding, Lester C., 166
Belitz, Mary, 165
Bell, Alexander Graham, 29
Bell, Bill, 180
Beloit, WI, 22
Benny, Jack, 68, 151, 168
Berry, Gov. Tom, 139
Bertsch, Garvin, 13
Betts, A. H., 151
Betts Grain Co., 151
Betts, Mark C., 39, 98
Betts, SD, 7, 52, 151, 154
Bismarck, ND, 44
Black Hills, 63, 137, 168
Blackman, Edwin, 39
Blendon postoffice, 7
Bobb, Dr. Byron A., 84, 107
Boehnen, Elsie, 142

Boehnen, Leo J., 142
Bond, Floyd, 87
Bon Homme County, 18, 19, 31
Bon Homme, DT, 17, 18
Borge, Victor, 76
Borglum, Gutzon, 68
Bottum, Joseph H., 159
Braase, Ordell, 163
Brady, Ezra M., 137
Brady, Msgr. John M., 160
Bramble County, 18
Bras, Harry L., 180
Braught, Jessie, 36
Breck, Pete, Sr., 166
Breese, Lou, 137
Bren, Joe, 132
Bridgewater, SD, 65, 165
Bromwell, Myrtle, 139
Brooks, Bob, 13
Brown County, 44
Brown, John, 21
Brown, Roy, 132
Browne, O. E., 167
Bruhn, Hans, 33
Bruhn, Lena, 33
Bruning, Charlotte, 13
Bryan, William Jennings, 58, 59, 61, 65, 66, 69, 157
Buck, Frank, 139
Buford Television, Inc., 151
Burg, John, 132
Burns, Lucy, 36
Burr, Dr. Chauncey S., 28, 162
Bush, Dr. William, 46
Butterfield's Department Store, 145

C

Cady, R. P., 19
Calhoun, Henry H., 46
Camp Cody, NM, 106, 107
Camp Greene, NC, 106
Canton, SD, 22, 44, 169
Capital (riverboat), 49
Carnegie, Andrew, 139
Carstens, George, 162
Carstens, Martha, 162
Case, U. S. Senator Francis H., 159, 169
Case, Leland D., 140
Cassem, Oscar E., 121
Centerville, SD, 139, 152
Chanka postoffice, 7
Chapin, Eugene Wilder, 61, 66
Chapin, Rev. M. E., 48
Chicago & North Western Railway, 60, 97, 154
Chicago, IL, 37, 59, 65, 167, 168
Chicago, Milwaukee & St. Paul Railway Co. (Milwaukee Road), 22, 23, 26, 27, 29, 36, 47, 51, 60, 84, 87, 95, 97, 109, 111, 116-118, 121, 141, 147, 153-155, 166, 167, 176, 183
Chicago, St. Paul, Minneapolis & Omaha Railroad (Omaha line), 97, 121, 146, 154, 183
Choteau Creek, 18
Christensen, Marlyn, 151
Christianer, Frank, 62
Civilian Pilot Training Program, 137
Civil War, 21, 22, 88
Clark, Charles Badger, Jr., 157
Clark, Rev. C. B., Sr., 158
Clark, Damon, 152
Cleveland, Pres. Grover, 57, 58
Coacher, William H., 144
Coca-Cola Bottling Company of Central South Dakota, 85, 97
Cody, Buffalo Bill, 157
Coffee Cup Cafe, 131
Collins, Dan, 79
Columbus, NM, 105
Commercial Hotel (Ethan), 40
Commerical (Savings) Bank, 1, 13, 25, 58, 85
Constable, Bill, 96
Coolidge, Pres. Calvin, 157
Coons, William W., 110
Corey, James, 37
Corker, Julius L., 8
Corn Belt Exposition, 7, 58, 59
Corn Belt Real Estate Association, 57, 58, 63
Cornell College (Iowa), 44
Corn Palace, 2, 7, 13, 14, 57-59, 61-63, 65-73, 75-77, 85, 96, 105, 106, 132, 137, 138, 140, 143-145, 149-153, 157, 167, 168, 179-182, 184, 186, 187
Corn Palace Relays, 164
Correll, Charles, 165
Coursey, Oscar W., 44, 150
Cox, William A., 25
Crow Creek Reservation, 157
Custer Battlefield Highway (U. S. 16), 4, 108, 153, 154
Custer, Lt. Col. George A., 22

D

Dakota Advocate, 28, 29
Dakota Central Telephone Co., 85
Dakota Mission Conference of Methodists, 43
Dakota Post, 169
"Dakota Queen" (airplane), 158, 159
Dakota Southern Railroad, 18
Dakota Territory, 17, 22, 27-31, 36, 43, 44, 162
Dakota Wesleyan University, 13, 44-47, 69, 107, 136-138, 140, 141, 149, 157-166, 169, 180, 181
Darwin, Australia, 143
Daughters of the American Revolution, 20
Davenport, Joseph L., 27, 29, 30
Davison, Alberta, 18
Davison County Normal Institute, 43
Davison County Tribune, 169
Davison, Henry C., 18, 192
Davison, Nathan L., 28
Davison, W. George, 28
Deadwood, SD, 157
Dean, Howard R., 106
DeBaugh's 20th Century Band, 59
Delaney, Dr. William A., Sr., 85, 107
Dell Rapids, SD, 84
Deming, NM, 106
DeSchepper, Dean L., 151
Devy, James D., 27
Dewey, William P., 19
Diamond Lake, IL, 158
Dillman, Will, 9
Dimock, SD, 146, 166
Dirty Thirties (Great Depression), 62, 72, 82, 113, 116, 131, 147, 151, 160
Dodd, Asa, 33
Dodd, Kate, 33
Dodd, Nellie, 33
Dorsey, Jimmy, 68
Dorsey, Tommy, 68
Doty, Wesley R., 144
Dougherty, Mary, 37
Dougherty, Michael, 37
Dousman, Nina S. (McBride), 79
Dowling, Al, 13
Duane, Ed, 168
Duncan, T. A., 45
Dundas, Dr. Robert F., 59, 63, 85
Dunham, Niles J., 184
Dunn, Harvey, 10
Durfee, Don, 72
Dwight, Harve, 36

E

Early, Jack, 180
Educator Supply Co., 180
Eilers, Carl, 22
Elce, Fred B., 85
Eliason, Martin K., 157
Elk Point, SD, 66, 163
Ellington, Duke, 68
Emsley postoffice, 7
Enchanted World Doll Museum, 179, 180
Enemy Creek, 112
Eppel, Raymond V., 151
Erie Telephone and Telegraph Co., 29
Erion Packing Co., 106, 179
Erpenbach, Alvin, 144
Ethan Commercial Club, 145
Ethan Creamery Co., 39
Ethan Enterprise, 112, 169, 184
Ethan, SD, 1, 7, 33, 39, 40, 48, 69, 83, 85, 89, 93, 94, 112, 116, 129, 131, 133, 136, 143, 149, 151, 154, 165-168, 181
Evanston, IL, 158

F

Farrar, Greg, 166
Fiji Islands, 143
Filkins, Sarah, 40
Firesteel Creek, 17, 19, 26, 30, 31, 112, 113, 122, 140
Firesteel, DT, 10, 17-23, 25, 26, 35, 36, 39, 43, 79, 105, 179
Firesteel Mail, 22
First National Bank, 28, 48, 79, 138
Foley and Devy saloon, 26
Food for Peace program, 159
Ford, Henry, 111
Ford, Tennessee Ernie, 68, 77, 150, 153
Forestburg, SD, 18
Fort Ord, CA, 142
Fort Thompson, 17
Fort Thompson Trail, 20, 35
Foss, Gov. Joe, 159
Foster, Fanny, 157
Foster, James S., 27-29
Fourth South Dakota Cavalry (Troop E), 105, 106, 110
Fourth South Dakota Infantry (Company F), 105-107, 110
Frankfort, SD, 44
Fraser, James Earle, 157, 162
Fremont, NE, 151
Friends of the Middle Border (Museum), 10, 13, 136, 140
Fullerton, George, 167
Fullerton, James, 167
Fullerton, Lumber Co., 167
Fullerton, Thomas, 59, 167
Fulmer, Darrell, 141
F. W. Woolworth Co., 163

G

Gabriel, Harold A., 144
Gale, Lawrence O., 26, 57-59, 62, 63, 65, 77
Gale, Theatre, 63, 112
Garey, Herman H., 39, 83, 90
Garland, Hamlin, 140
Garrett Theological Seminary, 158
George A. Hormel & Co., 179
Giese, John H., 82, 96
Giese Plumbing Co., 96, 103
Gillis, Cyrus W., 39
Gillis, Dr. Floyd D., 69, 107
Glum, Laura, 13
Goetsch, Herman A., 144
Goin, Clyde, 13
Goin, Mary, 13
Good Roads Fair, 62
Goodwin, Harold, 106
Goodykoontz, Stewart F., 26
Gosden, Freeman, 165
Goshen postoffice, 7
Grable, Betty, 153
Grand Army of the Republic, 88
Green Lantern Cafe, 131
Green, Richard L., 163
Greene, Edmonia, 21, 22
Greene, Frances, 17
Greene, Heman C., 17, 20-22, 27, 43
Greene Maj. Israel, 20-22, 25, 27
Greene, Louise (Hammer), 17
Greene, Gen. Nathaniel, 22
Greene, Theodore, 17
Griffith, Andy, 68
Grohs, Fred P., 85

H

Hain, Levi, 19
Hager, Mrs. Clarence, 160
Hager, Rev. Clarence E., 43
Hahn, Robert, 149
Haley and Lang Co., 127
Haley Neeley Wholesale Fruit Co., 127
Haflhide, Dr. M., 29
Hammer, Alson, 25, 30
Hammer, Frank, 25, 30
Hammer, Louise Greene, 17, 20, 21, 184
Hanson, County, 9, 18, 20, 35,
Hanson, Elsie Snow, 160
Hanson, Gloria Cofer, 13
Harmon, Leo, 166
Harper's Ferry Arsenal, 21
Haynes, Hip, 150
Haynes, James, 37
H. C. Davison & Co., 19
Head, John, 17, 19-21
Helgeland, Irma, 13
Helgeland, Pat, 13
Henricks, Gwenna, 13
Herbie Kay Orchestra, 69
Hersey, Harry B., 65
Hertz, Kelly, 13
Herzog, Louis, 29
Hess Rau and Co., 82
Hickey, William, 144
Hill, Mrs. W. S., 109

Mitchell's Main Street, brightly lit for the Christmas season, has been the scene of parades, carnivals and Corn Palace festivities for more than a century. Mitchell Area Historical Society/Clyde Goin photo.

Immensely heavy and structurally dangerous concrete domes on the third Corn Palace were replaced with lighter fiberglass minarets made by the O. L. Bussmus Construction Company. They relieved the roof of some 75 tons of dead weight. Clyde Goin photo.

Hisel, Bryan, 180
Hitchcock, Abner E., 46, 47, 81
Hitchcock, U. S. Senator Herbert E., 139, 159
Hitchcock Park, 168, 181
Hohn, William, 129
Holy Family Parish and Church, 43, 52, 97, 107, 138, 160
Homestead Act of 1862, 7
Honolulu, HI, 142
Hoover, Pres. Herbert, 68, 157
Hope, Bob, 68, 76
Hopkins, James D., 13
Howe, Oscar, 68, 72, 138, 157
Hoyt, Rev. Melancthon, 43
Hughes County, 60
Hunt, James C., 13
Huron College, 166
Huron, SD, 29, 44, 110, 136, 140, 157
Hutchinson County, 18, 31

I

Improved Sausage Co., 112
Industrial Workers of the World, 107, 118
Ingham, Cyrus B., 22
Ink, Clate, 105
International Hotel (Springfield), 18
Interstate Artificial Rain Co., 167
Interstate 90, 7, 154, 168
Isaac Spears Ice Co., 119
Italian Banda Rosa, 63
Ives, Burl, 77

J

James, Harry, 68, 153
James, (Jim) River, 5, 9, 10, 17, 22, 25-27, 35, 40, 41, 49, 87, 91, 112, 121, 181
Jamestown, ND, 18
Jefferson, SD, 163
Jencks, Maurice, W., 63
Jenks, Leon W., 168
Jensen, Nels, 113
J. F. Anderson Lumber Co., 48, 103
Jim River Advocate, 22
Jimtown Trail, 18, 20
Johnson, Fred M., 82
Johnson, Will, 82
Johnston, Edward S., 37, 38
Jolson, Al, 112, 165
Jones, Isham, 137
Jordan, Hazel, 13
Jorgenson, Karen, 13
Joseph and Jennie Robbie Sports Complex, 160

K

Kansas City Athletics, 163
Karolevitz, Bob, 192
Karolevitz, Phyllis, 13
Kay, Herbie, 137
Kearney, William, 72
Kehler, Charles, 145
Kehler, Mollie, 145
Kelley, Celia M., 162
Kelley, William, 162
Kennedy, Pres. John F., 159
Kerr, E. D., 158
KGDA Radio, 150, 152, 163
Kibbee, Howard R., Sr., 1, 85
Kienast, Kurt, 167
King, Karl L., 68
King, Nellie, 39
King, Theodore F., 94
Kings, Andrew J., 58, 63, 138, 143, 144
Kings, Floyd F., 61, 72, 138
Kingsbury County, 36
Kingsbury, George W., 19
King Sisters, 68
Kirkwood, Robert C., 163
KMHK Radio, 151
Knight, Rhoda, 40
Knowles, William H., 81
Korn Palace Broadcasting, Inc., 151
KORN Radio-TV, 151
Kotbra, Mary E., 162
Kratz, W. C., 29
Krueger, R. F., 29
Kuchera, Debra, 13
KXON-TV, 151

L

LaBarre, Arad J., 27
Lackey, Bill, 10
Lake Mitchell, 113, 120, 122, 137, 150, 152, 180, 191
LaMotte, Dedrick, 76
LaMotte, Susan, 76
Landmark Hotel, 179
Lawler, Hotel, 179
Lawler, John D., 23, 43, 58, 79-81, 85
Layton, William, 29
Lee, Brenda, 77
Lee, Lt. Col. Robert E., 21
Lee, Robert H., 83
Lehman, Diane, 13
Leslie, James, 29
Lewis, Henry N. 79
Lindbergh, Charles A., 111
Lindsey, John, 149
Litttle, Rich, 76
Logan, Jeff, 13
Logan, Nelson, 133, 136, 139
Lombardo, Guy, 68
Loomis Elevator Co., 84
Loomis, L. N., 84
Loomis, SD, 7, 35, 52, 84, 85, 88, 89, 152, 154
Lovejoy, Elijah P., 22
Lovre, Harold O., 159
Lowell, Luke W., 19
Luther, Jacob, 26
Lynn, MA, 58
Lyric Theatre, 112, 131, 133

M

Marion Junction, 22
Martin, Dick, 163
Marty, Bishop Martin, 43
Masters, Frankie, 137
Mayo, Mrs. Walter, 85
McBride, John, 79
McBride, Robert H., 79-81, 83, 85
McComish, Tom, 125
McEwen, Elbridge, 41
McEwen, Orlando, 41
McGovern, Eleanor, 159
McGovern, George S., 158-160
McGovern, Rev. Joseph, 159
McGovern, P. T. 27
McIntyre, Leo, 112
McKinley, Pres. William J., 157
McLaird, James D., 13
McLeod's Printing Co., 180
McMahon, Robert F., 143, 144
McMasters, Gov. William H., 68
Mead, George, 18
Mellette, Gov. Arthur C., 37
Merrill, Bishop S. M., 44
Metcalf, Roy, 84
Methodist Hospital, 101, 108, 118, 160, 180
Metropolitan Theatre, 112, 133
Meyer, Cletus, 144
Meyer, Francis, 144
Meyer, Louis, 144
Miami Dolphins, 160
Mickelson, Gov. George S., 163
Miles, Jerome, 39, 40
Mills Brothers, 76
Miner County, 18, 20
Minneapolis, MN, 63, 160
Mississippi River, 22
Missouri River, 17, 22, 26, 144
Mitchell, Alexander, 23, 29
Mitchell Area Arts Council, 139
Mitchell Area Historical Society, 1, 13, 184
Mitchell Baseball Association, 138
Mitchell Board of Trade, 28, 57
Mitchell Bottling Works, 85, 97
Mitchell Broadcasting Association, 151
Mitchell Business College, 171, 181
Mitchell Business Men's League, 63
Mitchell Capital, 19, 25, 29, 143, 167, 169
Mitchell Chamber of Commerce, 13, 57, 109, 141, 180
Mitchell Country Club, 118
Mitchell Daily Republic (Republican), 13, 29, 59, 111, 131, 132, 136, 137, 142, 143, 154, 160, 168, 169, 180, 184
Mitchell Elks Lodge, 96, 138
Mitchell Exchange Bank, 26
Mitchell Fire Department, 41, 47, 60, 83
Mitchell Gazette, 27, 39, 65, 152, 169, 184
Mitchell High School, 44, 48, 50, 55, 138, 157-159, 163, 164, 171, 172
Mitchell Iron and Supply Co., 32
Mitchell Kernels and Lady Kernels, 66, 163, 164, 166, 175, 181, 183
Mitchell Kiwanis Club, 108
Mitchell Lions Club, 141
Mitchell Mail, 79-81, 83, 85
Mitchell Municipal Airport, 145
Mitchell Power Co., 85
Mitchell Prehistoric Indian Village, 141, 180
Mitchell Printing Co., 143, 180
Mitchell Produce Co., 144
Mitchell Public (Carnegie) Library, 13, 138, 139
Mitchell Rotary Club, 110
Mitchell, SD, 1, 7, 8, 13, 14, 17-19, 25-31, 33, 35-37, 39-41, 43-48, 51-53, 57-63, 65, 66, 69-71, 76, 79, 80, 82-85, 87, 88, 91, 95-98, 100, 105-108, 111-113, 115, 117-119, 125, 131-133, 136-145, 147, 149, 151-155, 157-160, 162-168, 173, 176, 178-181, 183, 186, 190, 191
Mitchell Steam Laundry, 125
Mitchell Street and Interurban Railroad, 121
Mitchell Vocational Technical Institute, 162, 181
Mizener, David A., 25
Monmouth, IL, 57
Morgan, Scott, 166
Morris, Rev. John, 20
Morris Run, 112
Morriston postoffice, 7
Morrow, J. T., 1, 85
Moses, Frederic E., 25, 184
Mount Rushmore, 7
Mount Vernon Cooperative Creamery, 83, 94
Mount Vernon Fire Department, 45, 81
Mt. Vernon Gazette, 36-38
Mount Vernon, IA, 44
Mount Vernon Merchandise Co., 83
Mount Vernon Milling Co., 83
Mount Vernon Mustangs, 165
Mount Vernon News, 39, 83, 169, 184
Mount Vernon School, 49
Mount Vernon SD, 7, 33, 36-41, 43, 48, 50, 83-85, 90, 92, 96, 98, 105, 107, 110, 111, 114, 131, 132, 136, 139, 143, 144, 150, 151, 153, 154, 167, 168, 171, 181
Mount Vernon Telephone Co., 83
Mundt, U. S. Senator Karl, 159
Munsen, Gary, 166, 175
Music Corporation of America, 132
Musil, John, 98
Musil, Julia, 98
Muskogee, OK, 158
Mutual Broadcasting Co., 151

N

Nabors, Jim, 76
Nation, Carrie, 157
National Refining Co., 128
National Sheriff Association, 162
National Youth Administration, 145
Navin Hotel, 131
Nelings, Nellie, 31
New Deal, 131, 132, 135, 137-139, 145, 149
Nichol, Fred, 137, 159
Nicolls-Kress Pharmacy, 112
Nixon, Pres. Richard M., 159, 160
Norbeck, Gov. Peter, 13, 139, 140
Nordland, DT, 36
Northern Normal College, 166
Northwestern Public Service Co., 190
Northwestern University, 158, 159
Norton, S., 22
Notre Dame Academy, 106
Notre Dame Comets, 165, 174
Notre Dame High School, 174, 181
Notre Dame Junior College, 181

O

Oakley, Annie, 157
Oakland A's, 163
Obrembt, Ben, 166
O'Dell, Abe W., 30
Odessa (Devil's Lake), DT, 44
O'Flaherty, Rev. Colman, 107
O. L. Bussmus Construction Co., 187
Old Settlers' Day (Mount Vernon), 105, 110, 111
Olson, Bethilda, 106
Olson, Johnny, 150
109th Quartermaster Regiment (Medical Detachment), 143
147th Field Artillery Band, 132, 142
147th Field Artillery Regiment (Battery B), 142
Opiola, Michael E., 151
Ordway, DT, 44

Ordway, Gov. Nehemiah G., 44
Oscar Howe Art Center, 13, 139
Oster, Devonia, 13
Oster, Tony, 13
Over, W. H., 141
Owens, Ruth Bryan, 68

P

Page, Patti, 68
Panic of 1893, 58
Paramount Theatre, 133
Parker, SD, 43
Payne, Mark, 166
Pearl Harbor, 142, 144
Pease, John, 36
Pennington, Gov. John J., 19
Perry, Commodore Matthew C., 21
Perry Township, 40, 112
Peters, Fritz, 23
Peterson, Robert, 139
Phelps, Charles, 40
Phelps, Jerry, 167
Philippine Islands, 142
Phinney, Prof. Paul P., 58
Pierce, John T., 79
Pierre, SD, 13, 59-63, 71, 139, 145, 162
Plankinton, SD, 57, 79
Plante, Julius, 87
Platt, Joseph, 19
Pollard, Vincent, 107
Porter, Dr. Richard I., 13
Pound, McKinley, 144
Powell, Rev. David, 94
Prairie Market, 180
Presentation Junior College, 181
Presentation Sisters, 84, 101
Prohibition Party, 66
Provo, SD, 149
Ptak, Steve, 132
Pyle, Gladys, 140

Q

Queen of Peace Hospital, 101, 180
Quintal, Arthur A. (Joe), 163, 164, 171, 181

R

Rand, Sally, 168
Randall, F. Dwain (Doc), 180
Randall Foods, Inc., 180
Randall, Ron, 180
Rapid City, SD, 81
Red Cross, 109, 145, 152
Redfield, SD, 44, 65
Reese, Eunice, 179
Reese, Sheldon F., 179
Reierson, Art, 105
Reierson, Oscar, 105
Reitzel, Rev. John R., 43
Reitzel, Dr. Raymond J., 40, 184
Revolutionary War, 22, 39
Rew, Arthur C., 151
Rew, George H., 1, 85
Robbie, Joe, 160
Robinson, Myrtle, 139
Robinson, R. T., 40
Robinson, Will G., 144
Rochester, MN, 17
Rock Island, IL, 145
Rockport, DT, 22, 26, 49
Rohe, Col. Alexander, 58, 69
Rome, DT, 7, 39, 105
Ronald, Florence K., 160
Ronald, Malcolm B., 136, 137, 160
Ronald, William R., 131, 142
Roosevelt, Pres. Franklin D., 131, 132, 146
Roosevelt, Pres. Theodore, 66, 157
Rosenquist, Ole, 39
Rosenquist, Swan, 33
Ross Laboratories, 180
Rowan, Dan, 163
Rowley, Capt. Earl B., 105
Rowley, Mrs. George, 168
Rowley, Myron H., 25
Roxy Theatre, 133, 136, 138-140
Royal Neighbors of America, 116
Rozum, A. J. (Tony), 116, 132
Rozum, Charles, 13
Rozum Motor Co., 125, 132, 144, 166, 173
Rural Electrification Administration, 149

S

St. Joseph's Hospital, 72, 84, 100, 101, 108, 180
San Benito, TX, 105
Sanborn County, 164
Sanborn County Herald, 65
Scallin, Stephen F., Sr., 149
Scholfield, Thomas, 41
Schultz, Cal, 72
Schwann's Sales Enterprises, 180
Scotland, SD, 39
Scott, Lewis E., 90
Scott, Wally, 13
Security State Bank (Ethan), 89
Shakespeare, William, 154
Shevlin, Maurice (Mo), 174
Singing Young Americans, 150, 153
Sioux City Army Air Base, 145
Sioux City, IA, 18, 57, 58, 80, 139, 167, 180
Sioux Falls Argus-Leader, 66, 181
Sioux Falls, SD, 29, 40, 149, 150, 152, 154, 172, 181
Sioux Falls Press, 59, 131
Sisseton, SD, 160
Sitting Bull, 157
Skelton, Red, 68, 69, 77, 168
Smiley, Bernice Brown, 139
Smiley, Dr. John T., 143
Smiley, Dr. Thomas B., 105, 139
Smith, Bertha, 31
Smith, Hazel, 13
Smith, Henry S., 26
Smith, Jacob K., 25
Smith, William J., 94
Smith, William M., 65
Smithsonian Institution, 141
Snow, George W., 19
Soukup & Thomas International Balloon & Airship Museum, 178, 180
Sousa, John Philip, 2, 62, 63
South Dakota Farm Women's Congress, 162
South Dakota History, 83
South Dakota Home Guard (Company I), 107
South Dakota National Guard, 105, 142
South Dakota State Historical Society, 13, 184
South Dakota State College, 164
Southeastern Dakota Agricultural and Driving Park Association, 46, 57
Spanish-American War, 59, 150
Spencer, SD, 174
Spies, Burdell, 180
"Spirit of St. Louis" (airplane), 111
Springfield, SD, 18-20, 29, 192
Springfield Times, 19
Spry, George H., 79
Stair, Lawrence E., 43, 59, 91, 125
State Highway 37, 4, 140, 153
Stavig, Marvin L., 13
Steele, DT, 44
Stegeberg, Eleanor (McGovern), 158
Stewart, Jimmy, 145
Stickney, SD, 65
Stiles, Frank, 53
Stopfer, Henry, 129
Stover postoffice, 7
Stransky, John, 153
Stratford, NY, 17
Students' Army Training Corps, 107
Sud-Dakota Nachrichten, 169
Sullivan, Dan, 168
Summers George H., 32
Super City Shopping Center, 180
Swenson, Lyle W., 13, 162
Syncom, 180
Syracuse, NY, 28

T

Taft, Pres. William Howard, 58, 61, 65, 66, 157
Tatum, Dr. John, 168
Taylor, E. W., 27
Taylor, Vincent I., 144
Tessier's, Inc., 63
Thomsen, Gorden F., 180, 181
Thomson Newspapers, Inc., 160
3M Co., 180
Three Stooges, 68
Time Theatre, 133, 140
Timmins, Alice, 13
Timmins, William, 13
Tipton, W. E., 106
Tobin, Jim, 49
Toledo Linseed Oil Co., 57
Toshiba America Information Systems, Inc., 180
Trail King Industries, 180, 181
Traut, Jackie, 13
Truman, Pres. Harry, 146, 163
Turner, Produce Co., 147
Twelve Mile Creek, 112, 121
Tyndall, SD, 180

U

Uhre, Dale V., 144
Unitas, Johnny, 163
U. S. Army Air Corps, 136, 143, 144
U. S. Arsenal, 145
U. S. Land Office, 26
U. S. Marines, 21, 106
U. S. Topographical Engineers, 17
University of Michigan, 69
University of South Dakota, 141, 157, 163, 164
University of Wisconsin, 141

V

Van Eps, William, 22, 25
Vermillion, SD, 17, 46, 165, 168
Verschoor, John J., 133, 150
Victor postoffice, 7
Villa, Francisco (Pancho), 105
Village Bowl, 180
Vision 2000, 181

W

Walker, Edna, 106
Wallace, Henry, 132
Walrath, John O., 28
Walsh, John W., 22, 25, 27
Warne, Dr. Rodell C., 81, 84, 85
Warren, Lt. Gouveneur K., 17
Washington, George, 36
Waterloo, IA, 84
Watertown, SD, 144
Watkins, Ben, 36
Watkins, Evan D., 36
W. D. Anderson Mercantile (Mount Vernon), 139
Webber, Samuel, 1, 25, 29, 85
Weepie, Fred, 133, 168
Weepie's Hall (Ethan), 133, 168, 181
Welk, Lawrence, 68, 150, 153, 168
Wessington Springs, SD, 29
Western Chevrolet Co., 133
West Point Military Academy, 21
White, John R., 41, 184
Whiteman, Paul, 68, 168
White's Mill, 5, 10, 40, 41, 49
Whittier School, 31, 48, 157
Widmann, Fred, 37, 152
Widmann Hotel, 95, 149, 152, 179
Wieland, Cal, 154
Wilder, Laura Ingalls, 27
Willard A. Holbrook (ship), 142
William Galloway Co., 84
Williams, Andy, 68, 168
Williams, Emily, 40
Williams, Leonard B. (Bud), 162, 163, 166, 180
Wilson, Pres. Woodrow, 105
Wiltse, Jerome, 59
Wiltse, Rear Admiral Lloyd J., 143
Withers, Jane, 140
Wittenhagen, Wilbert O., 144
Women's Christian Temperance Union, 48, 66
Woods, Mabel O., 160
Woodward, C. B., 83
Woonsocket, SD, 65, 159
Works Progress Administration, 10, 135, 137-139, 141
World War I, 13, 72, 79, 95, 100, 106, 107, 111, 118, 125, 129, 136, 144, 160
World War II, 142, 144, 147, 151, 153, 155, 157-160, 162

Y

Yale Divinity School, 43
Yankton College, 137, 164, 165
Yankton Community Library, 13
Yankton High School, 66
Yankton, SD, 17-19, 29, 39, 40, 43, 44, 66, 150, 152
Yankton Press and Dakotaian, 79
Young, Barbara, 72
Young Men's Christian Association, 48, 162

Z

Zeal, Billie, 13
Zeal, Wally, 13
Zeier, Henry, 94
Zietlow, J. L. W., 85
Zweibrucken, Germany, 143

The pasque is South Dakota's official state flower which blooms each spring in isolated virgin prairie locations in Davison County. It is a symbol of the tenacity of those who settled the area and the native people who preceded them. Steve Laramore photo.

Power lines of the Northwestern Public Service Company formed an alley arcade from south to north across Mitchell's downtown, all the way to the Corn Palace. Dr. Richard I. Porter photo.

It has been said that Mitchell is "a town of straight-lined streets and straight-thinking people." The business district is centered in this late 1980s aerial photo, looking from south to north. Lake Mitchell is located in the upper left. Clyde Goin photo.

ABOUT THE AUTHOR

Bob Karolevitz has written more than 30 books and several thousand magazine and newspaper features during a writing career which has spanned five decades.

Among his wide range of titles are *Uniquely South Dakota*, with Bernie Hunhoff; *Challenge: The South Dakota Story; From Quill to Computer*, a history of community newspapers in the United States; *Yesterday's Motorcycles; Doctors of the Old West;* and *Where Your Heart Is*, the biography of Dakota-born artist Harvey Dunn which earned for him a coveted Wrangler award from the National Cowboy Hall of Fame and Heritage Center, Oklahoma City.

His humor books include *Tears in My Horseradish*, *Everything's Green But My Thumb* and *The Golfer's Good Book*.

Karolevitz is a native of Yankton, South Dakota, and a graduate in printing and rural journalism from South Dakota State College (now University). He also has a master's degree in journalism from the University of Oregon.

He is a veteran of World War II and the Korean conflict, having served as a division historian and public information officer among other duties.

He and his wife Phyllis reside at Cedar Crest Farm near Mission Hill, South Dakota, where he writes a weekly newspaper column and, as he says, will continue "to labor in the vineyard of words until they put me away."

Author Bob Karolevitz located the grave of Henry C. Davison, after whom Davison County was named, in the Springfield, South Dakota, cemetery. Davison, the subject of much historical misinformation, died in 1880 shortly before his 39th birthday. M. Jill Sundstrom photo.